Just Grammar

Elementary

Includes
Answer Key

Carol Lethaby
Ana Acevedo
Jeremy Harmer
with Cheryl Pelteret

Viva Books

New Delhi | Mumbai | Chennai | Kolkata | Bangalore | Hyderabad | Kochi | Guwahati

Photo acknowledgements
p.6 ©Corbis; p.10 a ©Rob Barker, b ©Rob Barker, c ©Lawrence Manning/Corbis, d ©Robert Garvey/Corbis, e © Apple Mackintosh, f ©Judith Collins/Alamy, g ©Burke/Triolo Productions/Jupiter Images/Brand X Alamy, h ©Helene Rogers/ Alamy, I ©Rob Wilkinson/Alamy. J, ©D. Hurst/Alamy; p. 12 I ©Sipa Press/Rex Features, r ©Allstar Picture Library/ Alamy; p. 13 ©Randy Faris/Corbis; p. 15 I © Jose Fuste Raga/Corbis, c ©Angelo Hornak/Corbis, r ©Iain Masterton/ Alamy; p. 16 ©Phil Wigglesworth/Alamy, p.19 ©Altrendo Images/Getty Images; p. 28 ©WizData Inc./Alamy; p.30 ©Corbis; p.34 ©Gaboria/Stockfolio/Alamy; p.36 ©Hoberman Collection/Corbis; p.40 ©Stuart Dee/Alamy; p.46 ©Reza Estakhrian/Stone/Getty Images; p.47 ©Helene Rogers/Alamy; p.51 ©Mika/zefa/Corbis; p.52 ©Christian Darkin/Alam; p. 63 ©Michael Prince/Corbis; p. 64 ©Reuters/Corbis, ©Colin Weston/Travel Ink/alamy, ©Richard Klune/Corbis; p.69 a ©Corbis, b ©Grace/zefa/Corbis, c ©Thinkstock Images/Alamy; p. 73 ©Georgina Bowater/Corbis; p.74 © Chloe Johnson/Alamy; p.76 ©Blend Images/Getty Images.

First Indian Edition 2009

VIVA BOOKS PRIVATE LIMITED

- 4737/23 Ansari Road, Daryaganj, New Delhi 110 002
  E-mail: vivadelhi@vivagroupindia.net, Tel. 42242200
- 76, Service Industries, Shirvane, Sector 1, Nerul, Navi Mumbai 400 706
  E-mail: vivamumbai@vivagroupindia.net, Tel. 27721273, 27721274
- Jamals Fazal Chambers, 26 Greams Road, Chennai 600 006
  E-mail: vivachennai@vivagroupindia.net, Tel. 28290304, 28294241
- B-103, Jindal Towers, 21/1A/3 Darga Road, Kolkata 700 017
  E-mail: vivakolkata@vivagroupindia.net, Tel. 22836381, 22816713
- 7, Sovereign Park Apartments, 56-58, K. R. Road, Basavanagudi, Bangalore 560 004
  E-mail: vivabangalore@vivagroupindia.net, Tel. 26607409, 26607410
- 101-102 Mughal Marc Apartments, 3-4-637 to 641, Narayanguda, Hyderabad 500 029
  E-mail: vivahyderabad@vivagroupindia.net, Tel. 27564481, 27564482
- First Floor, Beevi Towers, SRM Road, Kaloor, Kochi 682 018, Kerala
  E-mail: vivakochi@vivagroupindia.net, Tel: 0484-2403055, 2403056
- H. No. 12, P. B. Road, Near Arya Hospital, Rehabari, Guwahati 781 008
  E-mail: vivaguwahati@vivagroupindia.net, Tel: 0361-2735624

www.vivagroupindia.com

Published by arrangement with
Marshall Cavendish Education
119 Wardour Street
London W1F 0UW, UK

ISBN-10: 81-309-1107-8
ISBN-13: 978-81-309-1107-6

Published by Vinod Vasishtha for Viva Books Private Limited, 4737/23, Ansari Road, Daryaganj, New Delhi - 110 002. Printed and bound by Raj Press, R-3, Inderpuri, New Delhi - 110 012.

Contents

Introduction

To the student

Welcome *to Just Grammar*. You can use this book with other students and a teacher, or you can work alone with it.

In this book you will find clear explanations of the grammar you need at this level. There are examples to help you understand the explanations too. Each unit has exercises for you to practise the grammar points.

When you see this symbol ( ) it means that the answers to the practice exercises are in the Answer key at the back of the book. You can check your answers there.

You can look at the contents page to find the grammar you want to understand and practise.

We are sure that this book will help you to progress in English.

To the teacher

This book is part of a series designed to be used alone or to supplement any coursebook you may be using. Each book in the series specialises in either language skills or (as in the case of *Just Grammar*) in aspects of the English language. It can be used either in class or by students working on their own.

Just Grammar consists of 24 units which offer comprehensive grammar explanations, and provide practice activities to ensure the student's ability to use the language. Apart from the last two review units, the organisation is alphabetical. Users should look in the contents list on page 3 to see which area of grammar they wish to work on.

Students will be able to use *Just Grammar* without needing explanation or guidance on the part of the teacher. Having read through the explanations and examples in the book, they can do the exercises, and then check them in the comprehensive Answer key at the back. However, the units are also highly appropriate for work in class.

We are confident that you will find this book a real asset and we recommend that you also try the other books in the series: *Just Reading and Writing, Just Vocabulary* and *Just Listening and Speaking.*

UNIT 1

Adverbs of frequency

always usually often sometimes occasionally never

Most frequent → **Least frequent**

To talk about how often you do something, follow this pattern:

Affirmative			
Subject	**Frequency adverb**	**Verb**	
I	usually often never always sometimes occasionally never	play	soccer on Saturday.

*I **usually** play soccer on Saturday.*
*She **always** eats pizza on Sunday.*
*Paul and Mary **never** have hamburgers.*

***Yes/No* questions**				
Auxiliary verb	**Subject**	**Adverb**	**Verb**	
Do	you	always	play	soccer on Saturday?

*Does Ayesha **sometimes** go shopping? – Yes, she does.*
*Do you **often** go for a walk on Sunday? – Yes, I do.*
*Do they **occasionally** play tennis? – No, they don't.*

Questions with *How often ... ?*				
Question word	**Auxiliary verb**	**Subject**	**Verb**	
How often	do	you	play	soccer?

***How often** do your friends go to the cinema?*
***How often** does Ella go skiing?*

A frequency adverb can be a phrase:

every	week month day year

once twice three times four times etc.	a	week month day year

With a phrase, follow this pattern:

Subject	**Verb**		**Adverb**
I	play	soccer	**twice a month.**

*We go swimming **four times a week.***

Auxiliary verb	**Subject**	**Verb**		**Adverb**
Do	you	play	soccer	**every week?**

*Does Tom work out **every day?***
– Yes, he does.
*Do you go skiing **twice a year?***
– No, we don't.

1 Look at Susie's calendar and circle the correct answers.

a How often does Susie go swimming?

once a week / once a month

b How often does she go shopping?

once a month / twice a month

c How often does she go to the cinema?

twice a week / twice a month

Answer these questions.

d How often does she play tennis?

....

e How often does she work out?

....

S	M	T	W	Th	F	S
1 Play tennis	2	3 Swimming club	4 Work out	5 Work out	6 Cinema with Joe	7 Shopping (buy new bag!)
8 ~~Play tennis~~	9 Mum's birthday	10 Swimming club	11 Work out	12 Work out (take Emma)	13 Play tennis	14
15	16 ~~Interview~~	17 Swimming club	18 Work out	19 Work out	20	21 My birthday!
22	23 Cindy's back!	24 Swimming club	25 Work out	26 Work out	27 Cinema with ~~Joe~~ Cindy	28 Shopping
29 Play tennis (9.30!)	30	31 Swimming club (drink afterwards)	~~Work out~~			

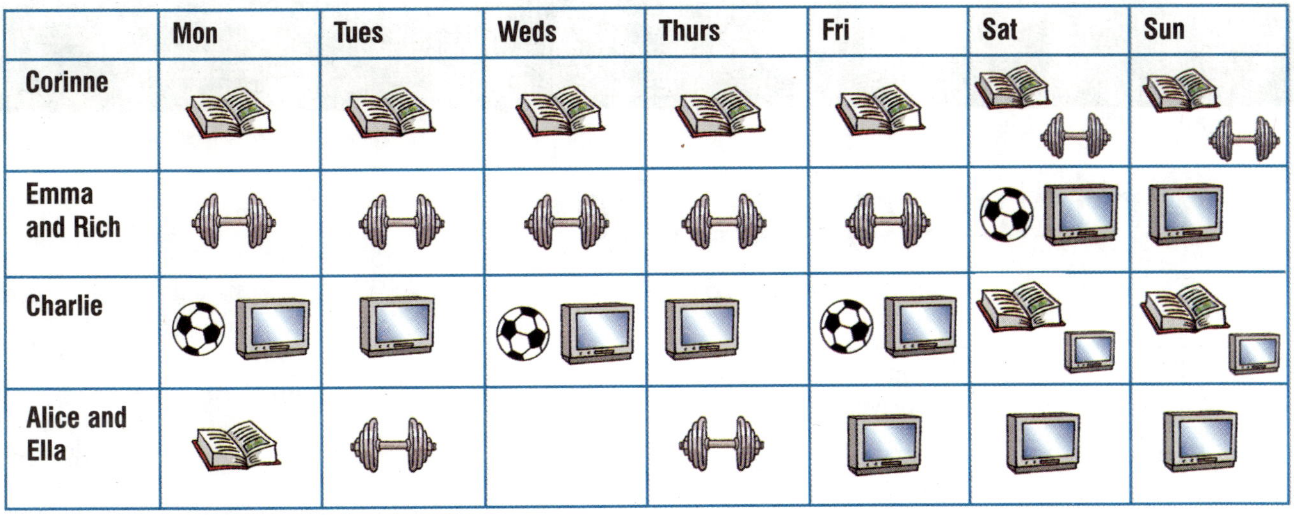

2 Look at the table and ask or answer the questions.

a How often does Corinne read?

b How often do Emma and Rich read?

c How often does Charlie play football?

d ……………………………………………?

Twice a week.

e ……………………………………………?

Never.

f ……………………………………………?

Three times a week.

g Who reads once a week?

h Who sometimes plays football?

i Who always watches TV?

j Who usually works out?

3 Put the words in the correct order to make questions and answer the questions about you.

a often / you / swimming / do / How / go / ?

b read / newspaper / How / you / do / often / the / ?

c homework / often / do / do / you / How / ?

d often / you / play / How / do / tennis / ?

e seaside / How / go / often / you / to / the / do / ?

f you / Do / day / work out / every / ?

g you / get up / at the weekend / late / Do / always / ?

UNIT 2

Articles: *a, an, the*

Indefinite articles

Paul's	a	doctor. taxi driver.
I'm	an	architect. engineer.

Always use an indefinite article to describe a person's job:

Jake's a nurse.

Don't use an article in the plural:

Jake and Simon are nurses.

Use *an* in front of a vowel:

*Sarah's **an** actor.*

Definite article

Note that *the* is a definite article. Use *the* to talk about something you or others know about:

*What colour's **the** Japanese flag?*
***The** capital of Belgium is Brussels.*
*That's my house – **the** house with **the** red door.*

1 Match the rules *a–d* with the example sentences *1–4*.

Rule

a We don't use an article in the plural.
b We use *the* to talk about something you or others know about.
c We use *a* or *an* to describe a person's job.
d We always use *an* in front of a vowel.

Example

1 Crete is an island in the Mediterranean.
2 My parents are teachers.
3 Paris is the capital of France.
4 He wants to be a doctor one day.

2 Complete the sentences with *a* or *an* only when necessary.

a Gill's ...*a*... singer.

b Bob's .... architect.

c Jamie and Ray are .... cooks.

d Tomoko's .... Japanese.

e Moira's .... engineer.

f Colin's .... computer programmer.

3 Look at the sentences in the box. Complete sentences *a–f* with *a*, *an* or Ø (= nothing).

Tom's a teacher.

Tom and Angela are teachers.

Don's an engineer.

Don and Vivian are engineers.

a My friends are .... actors.

b Claudio's .... computer programmer. Carla's .... computer programmer too.

c Are you .... nurses? – No, we aren't. I'm .... doctor and my friend's .... cook.

d What's your job? – I'm .... engineer.

e Really? I'm .... engineer too!

f Oh, so we are both .... engineers.

4 Complete the sentences with *a*, *an* or *the*.

A: Hello! Is this (**a**) ....the.... English class?

B: Yes. Are you (**b**) .... new girl from Poland?

A: Yes! My name's ....Anya.... . Are you (**c**) .... student too?

B: No, I'm not! I'm Miss White. I'm (**d**) .... English teacher for this class.

Come into (**e**) .... classroom and meet all (**f**) .... other students.

A: This is Luke. He's in (**g**) .... school basketball team!

Luke's (**h**) .... very good artist, too.

And he's in (**i**) .... school band as well.

B: Oh, (**j**) I'm in .... basketball team, too …

5 This is what Mark wants to buy at the shopping centre. Write *a*, *an* or Ø by the things in the shopping list.

a ...a... hamburger

b .... chips

c .... umbrella

d .... Australian flag

e .... iPod

f .... Russian doll

g .... Mexican hat

h .... CDs

i .... stamps

j .... T-shirt

6 Write occupations. Use *a*/*an*. Then write an example of people you know.

Example: An engineer – My friend's an engineer.
A doctor – Alan Ashby's a doctor.

....

....

....

....

UNIT 3

can, can't

Affirmative		
I You He/She/It We They	can	play the piano.

Negative		
I You He/She/It We They	cannot (can't)	play the guitar.

Interrogative		
Can	I you he/she/it we they	play the drums?

Short answers					
Affirmative			**Negative**		
Yes,	I you he/she/it we they	can.	No,	I you he/she/it we they	can't.

Use *can*
– to talk about ability:
*I **can** play the piano.*
– to give permission:
*You **can** watch TV for two hours.*

Note that *can* is invariable (it doesn't change with the subject):
*I **can** play the clarinet.*
*Becky **can** play the saxophone.*
*We **can** play the drums.*

1 Look at this table and complete the questions and answers below.

Jay	✗	✔	✗	✗	✗	✔
Maggie	✗	✔	✔	✗	✗	✗
Mike	✔	✗	✗	✔	✔	✗
Helena	✔	✗	✗	✔	✗	✔

a Can........ Jay play the keyboard? – No, he can't.
b .... Maggie play the guitar? – ....
c .... Mike sing? – ....
d .... Helena read music? – ....
e Jay .... the guitar.
f Maggie .... sing.
g Mike .... the drums.
h Helena .... dance.

2 Jay, Maggie, Mike and Helena are in a band. Answer these questions. Say why.

a Who plays the guitar?

I think Jay plays the guitar, because he can play the guitar but he can't sing.

b Who plays the drums?

....

c Who plays the keyboards?

....

d Who is the singer?

....

e Who writes the songs?

....

3 Write questions and answers.

a Ronaldinho / play football ✓ Can Ronaldinho play football? Yes, he can.
b Ahmed's mother / play the piano ✗ ....
c dogs / swim ✓ ....
d a cheetah / run fast ✓ ....
e your parents / dance the tango ....
f you draw / well ....
g you send / a text message ....
h you speak / French ....
i you count / to 100 in English ....
j you ride / a motorbike ....

4 Read this paragraph about Stevie Wonder and complete the table about him.

Stevie Wonder is one of the most famous musicians of all time, and what is most interesting is that he can't see – Steveland Morris (his real name) is totally blind. Stevie is an amazing musician: he can play the keyboards (piano and synthesizer), the drums, the bass guitar and the harmonica, but he can't play the trumpet, the cello or the violin.

Stevie Wonder

can	can't
....	....
....	....
....	....

5 Look at this information about Paul McCartney and write a paragraph about him.

can	can't
play keyboards, guitar, drums	trumpet, saxophone, violin

....

....

....

....

6 Read the poster and complete the sentences below.

a Joe can sing, but he ...can't... dance.

b He .... play a musical instrument.

c Joe, Sandra and Harry .... all sing.

d Sandra and Harry .... read music, but Joe ....

e Nobody .... play the ....

f Harry and Sandra .... play a musical instrument.

g They .... write songs, but Joe ....

Do you want to be in our own 'High School Musical'?

Can you...?

sing	Joe Sandra Harry
dance	Harry Sandra
write songs	Joe
play:	
	Harry
	Sandra

read music	Sandra Harry

Come to our first practice this afternoon in the school hall!

7 Now fill in the application form. Which of the things in the poster can you do? Which can't you do?

Application form for High School Musical

Name:...

....

Age:...

....

....

....

....

....

....

UNIT 4

Comparative adjectives

To compare things or people, follow these patterns:

Adjectives of one or two syllables			
	adjective + *-er*		
Linda is	funnier taller happier	than	me. Gina. you. her.

You are tall, but Linda is taller ***than*** *you.*
Gina is funny, but Linda is funnier ***than*** *Gina.*

Adjectives of two or more syllables			
	more + adjective		
Museums are	more interesting more boring more expensive	than	parks. restaurants.

Museums are ***more*** *interesting* ***than*** *parks.*
Yes, but museums are ***more*** *expensive* ***than*** *parks.*

To compare things or people that are similar, follow this pattern:

Marla	is isn't	as	funny tall happy interesting boring	as	Linda. us. them. him. her sister.

Linda is funny.
Yes, but Marla is funny too – she is ***as*** *funny* ***as*** *Linda.*

Note some different forms and spellings.
Short adjectives ending in *-y*:
happy – ***happier***
pretty – ***prettier***

One-syllable adjectives ending in one vowel + one consonant:
big – ***bigger***
hot – ***hotter***

Short adjectives ending in *-e*:
nice – ***nicer***

Irregular forms:
good/well – ***better***
bad – ***worse***

1 Match the beginnings and ends of the rules.

Comparatives: rules

a To compare similar things …
b The comparative of adjectives of one or two syllables is …
c The comparative form of adjectives of two or more syllables is …
d When an adjective ends in y …
e When a one-syllable adjective ends in one vowel + one consonant …

1 *more* + adj + *than.*
2 we double the last letter.
3 we use *as* … *as.*
4 adj + *-er* + *than.*
5 we change the *y* for an *i* and add *-er.*

2 Complete the sentences with the phrases in the box and the information below.

Tom – 1.80m/70kg Dick – 1.80m/70kg Harry – 1.85m/65kg

as tall as
more interesting than
taller than as modern as
as thin as thinner than
more modern than
as interesting as

a Tom's ......as tall as...... Dick. (tall)
b Harry's .... Dick and Tom. (tall)
c Tom's .... Dick. (thin)
d Harry's .... Dick and Tom. (thin)

The Miho Museum, Kyoto (opened1997)
The Guggenheim Museum, Bilbao (opened 1997)
Tate Modern, London (opened 2000)

e The Miho Museum is .... the Guggenheim, Bilbao. (modern)
f Tate Modern is .... the other two museums. (modern)
g The Miho Museum is .... the Guggenheim, Bilbao. (interesting)

3 Look at the completed sentences in Activity 2. When do we use *-er than*? When do we use *more ... than*?

The Guggenheim, Bilbao

The Tate Modern, London

The Miho Museum, Kyoto

4 Complete the sentences with the correct comparative forms. Use the comparative form (+ adjective) or *as ... as* (= adjective).

a Beaches are (+ exciting) ......more exciting than...... mountains.
b The internet is (+ useful) .... an encyclopaedia.
c I don't think so. Encyclopaedias are (= useful) ......as useful as...... the internet.
d Is your hair (= short) .... mine, Jill?
e Don't be silly. My hair's (+ short) .... yours.
f Canada's (+ big) .... Australia.
g Helen's story's (+ interesting) .... yours.
h Maybe. But my story's (+ long) .... Helen's.
i Madonna's new CD is just (= good) .... all her other CDs.
j No, it isn't. It's (+ good) .... all her other CDs.

5 Write the names of two places or people in your country. Then compare them.

The Natural History Museum is more interesting than the Transport Museum.

a an interesting museum
b a beautiful woman
c a high mountain
d handsome man
e a wide river
f a boring book

6 Complete the advert with the correct comparative forms.

Going on a skiing holiday?

Imagine the perfect holiday: the flight is (**a**) (+ short) shorter than your journey to work. The hotel is (**b**) (= comfortable) .... your own home. The mountains are (**c**) (+ beautiful) .... the pictures in the brochure. Skiing is (**d**) (+ easy) .... walking. You're a natural. You're (**e**) (= fast) .... the wind down the mountain. But accidents happen: you fall and break your leg. A night in hospital can be (**f**) (+ expensive) .... a night in a luxury hotel. Travel insurance isn't (**g**) (= expensive) .... you think. *Getaround* travel insurance. It's (**h**) (+ cheap) .... a meal out.

7 Write comparative sentences. Use adjectives from the box.

beautiful	handsome	long
tall	narrow	wide	high
small	big	young	old

a The Amazon, Brazil
The Thames, England
The Amazon is wider than the Thames.
The Thames isn't as wide as the Amazon.

b The Great Pyramid of Cheops, Egypt
The Eiffel Tower, Paris
....
....

c The European continent
The American continent
....
....

d Brad Pitt
George Clooney
....
....

e Angelina Jolie
Scarlet Johansson
....
....

UNIT 5

Countable and uncountable nouns

Countable nouns are nouns that can be counted and have a plural form:
one egg, two eggs

Uncountable nouns are nouns that cannot be counted and have no plural form:
sugar, milk, bread

Sometimes the same noun can be countable and uncountable:
*I like **chicken** for lunch.* (uncountable)
*There are 50 **chickens** on the farm.* (countable)

Use the indefinite article *a/an* with singular countable nouns:
*I'd like **a** shirt.* (singular noun)
*I want to buy **a** suit.* (singular noun)

Use *some* with uncountable nouns and plural nouns:
*I want to buy **some** shoes.* (plural noun)
*He needs **some** eggs.* (plural noun)
*I'd like **some** coffee.* (uncountable noun)

To ask about price, use *How much is ... ?* with singular and uncountable nouns:
***How much is** this tie? – It's £20.* (tie = singular noun)
***How much is** this sugar? – It's £3 a kilo.* (sugar = uncountable noun)

Use *How much are ... ?* with plural nouns:
***How much are** these shoes? – £100* (shoes = plural noun)

To ask about quantity, use *How much ... ?* with uncountable nouns:
***How much cheese** do you want? – About 400g, please.*

Use *How many ... ?* with countable nouns:
***How many bananas** do you want? – Four, please.*

1 Write the phrases in the correct column.

three tomatoes   sandwiches   a banana   bread   coffee
sugar   some meat   some chicken   an egg   cheese

Countable nouns

three tomatoes ....
....
....
....

Uncountable nouns

bread ....
....
....
....
....
....

2 Choose the correct answer for these questions: *six / 500g*.

a How much cheese do you want? 500g
b How many eggs do you want? ....
c How much sugar do you want? ....
d How many bananas do you want? ....
e How many sandwiches do you want? ....
f How much meat do you want? ....

3 Look at the food in the picture. Write questions with *How much* or *How many*. Then choose the best answer from the box.

1

2

3

4
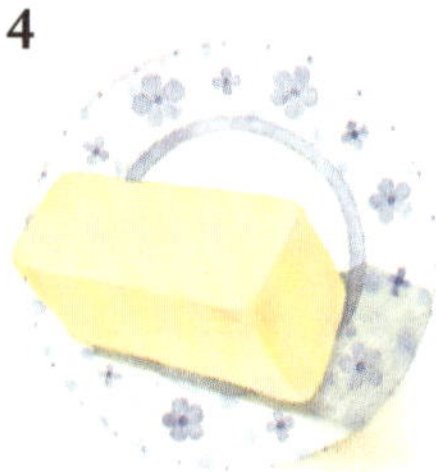
5 6

a bottle	about five	some	eight	a bowl	some

a How many eggs are there? ....eight........

b .... flour .... ? ....

c .... cheese .... ? ....

d .... butter .... ? ....

e .... tomatoes .... ? ....

f .... oil .... ? ....

4 Ask and answer questions about this food.

1 1lb cheese for £4

2 milk at only 50p a litre

3 eggs at only £1 per dozen

4 salad at £1.50 a bag

a Ask and answer about price

1 Q: How much is that cheese?

2 ....

3 ....

4 ....

b Ask about quantity

1 Q: How much cheese do you want?

2 ....

3 ....

4 ....

5 Now complete these dialogues.

a WOMAN: Hello. I'd like ....some cheese...., please.

ASSISTANT: Certainly, how .... do you want?

WOMAN: How .... ?

ASSISTANT: £5.50 a pound.

WOMAN: I'll take half a pound please.

ASSISTANT: Here you are. That's £2.25, please.

WOMAN: Thanks.

b MAN: I need ....

ASSISTANT: How .... ?

MAN: Just a dozen, please.

ASSISTANT: OK. Anything else?

MAN: No, thanks. How .... ?

ASSISTANT: £1.50, please.

MAN: There you are.

ASSISTANT: Thanks.

6 Read the recipe and complete the dialogue.

g = grams   ml = millilitres

PANCAKES

Ingredients
2 eggs
250g flour
125g butter
300ml milk

Ideas for fillings: cheese, chicken, sugar with lemon juice.

A: Let's make pancakes!
B: OK! But what do we need?
A: Well, we need .... Look at the recipe. .... eggs do we need?
B: We need .... eggs. And we need flour.
A: .... flour do we need?
B: ....
A: We need .... butter, too, don't we? .... butter do we need?
B: ....
B: What about milk? .... milk do we need?
A: Um ... we need .... of milk.
B: What fillings can we put in the pancakes?
A: Well, we've got .... cheese, and .... chicken ...
B: And we've got .... sugar, and .... lemon juice.
A: Sounds delicious!

7 Complete the questions. Then answer the questions about yourself.

a How ....many.... hours do you sleep every night? ....
....
b How .... water do you drink every day?
....
c How .... fruit do you eat in a week?
....
d How .... coffee do you drink a day?
....
e How .... money do you spend on food every month?
....

UNIT 6

Demonstrative adjectives

	Singular	Plural
Close	this	these
Distant	that	those

You can use the demonstratives *this*, *that*, *these*, *those* as adjectives or as pronouns.

Adjectives:

These books are new.

That computer is old.

Pronouns:

This is my cousin Jim.

Those are my keys.

Use *this* and *these* for what is close:

Look at this book on the desk.

Use *that* and *those* for what is distant:

Look at those photos on the wall.

1 Fill in the blanks with *this*, *that*, *these* or *those*.

2 Read the dialogues and circle the correct word.

A: Who's *this* / *these*, Cynthia?
B: *These* / *That's* my grandmother. It's a very old photo!
A: She's beautiful and I love the clothes.

A: Hey. Are *these* / *this* your new drawings?
B: Yes, they are. Don't look! They're not very good.

A: *Those* / *That's* an interesting photo. Who is it?
B: I'm not sure. Let's go and see.

A: *That* / *Those* books are for students.
B: And *these* / *that* computer? Is it for students too?
A: Yes, everything in *that* / *this* room is for students.

A: Mummy, mummy. Look at *this* / *those* people! They're funny!
B: No, darling. They're not funny. And don't point.

A: Are *this* / *those* clothes in the sale, too?
B: No, *these* / *those* aren't in the sale. But *those* / *that* clothes near you are in the sale.

3 Complete the conversations with *this (is)*, *that('s)*, *these* or *those*.

A: What's (**a**) .... ?

B: What – (**b**) .... building over there? (**c**) .... a new hotel.

A: What's (**d**) .... ?

B: I don't know, but I think it's very old.

A AND B: Hello, Laura! Are (**e**) .... your children?

B: Yes! (**f**) .... Rob, and (**g**) .... is Sophie. Children, (**h**) .... are my friends from university, Zoe and Matt.

A: I don't really like (**i**) ....

B: No, they're a bit big. What about (**j**) .... over there?

A: Mmm, I like (**k**) .... white jeans …

B: Excuse me, have you got (**l**) .... in other sizes? They're for my friend. (**m**) .... her, by the mirror.

B: Do you like (**n**) .... colour? They don't have (**o**) .... jeans in white, in your size.

A: Oh, (**p**) .... a pity. I don't really like red …

UNIT 7

going to future: affirmative, negative and *yes/no* questions

Affirmative				
I	am ('m)	going to	get a job	(soon).
He She It	is ('s)			
You We They	are ('re)			

Negative			
I	am not ('m not)	going to	look for a job.
He She It	is not (isn't)		
You We They	are not (aren't)		

Use *going to* future
– to talk about plans and intentions:

__I'm going to__ buy a camera tomorrow.
__He isn't going to__ get a job.
__We're going to__ go on holiday next week.

– to make predictions:

__It's going to__ rain on Sunday.
__You're going to__ fall.
__They aren't going to__ travel.

Use a form of the verb *be* in short answers after *yes/no* questions:

Are you going to get up early? – __Yes, I am.__
Is she going to get married? – __No, she isn't.__
Are they going to buy a new car? – __Yes, they are.__

After verbs like *think* and *hope*, you can use *that*, but you don't have to:

Do you think (__that__) he's going to study?
I hope (__that__) it isn't going to rain.
I don't think (__that__) they're going to come.

1 Read the statements about the picture. True (T) or False (F)?

a All the sentences are about the future. T
b The people know what is going to happen.
c The people are guessing what is going to happen.
d The man plans to finish today.
e All the sentences have a form of the verb *be*.
f The question begins with *going to*.
g The man is going to work on the bridge again tomorrow.

2 Write sentences for the pictures *a–d*. Use *going to* with the verbs.

a

it/rain

b

I/be

c

I/have

d

they/crash

a It's going to rain.
b ....
c ....
d ....

3A Read the notes from the meeting of the Castle Canoe Club. Complete the questions and write short answers.

Minutes of meeting: 12 June
Present: All members

The main item on the agenda was the trip to SW Scotland in August. We decided to make a list of things we are going to do, and who is going to do each one:

1 Collect money from the 25 members interested in this trip
Rachel
2 Phone Loch Keel Canoe Club about camping there
Tom
3 Find out about canoes we can use at Loch Keel
Hannah
4 Book tents online from Tenthire.com
Ben
5 Collect tents
Kieran and Rory
6 Discuss transport for some of our own canoes
Will
7 Write to local newspapers
Kate, Jamie, Hannah
8 Contact *Watersports Weekly* about a possible interview
Jamie

a Is Rachel going to find out about canoes they can use? No, she isn't.
b .... Tom .... book the tents? ....
c .... Kieran and Rory .... collect the tents? ....
d .... Will .... contact *Watersports Weekly*? ....
e .... Tom and Will .... write to the local newspapers? ....
f .... Kate .... find out about canoes at Loch Keel? ....

3B Now write correct sentences for the negative answers.

a Rachel is going to collect money from the 25 members interested in this trip.
b ....
c ....
d ....
e ....
f ....

UNIT 8

going to future: interrogative

Interrogative			
Am	I	going to	be late?
Is	he she it		
Are	you we they		

Short answers					
Affirmative			**Negative**		
Yes,	I	am.	No,	I	am not. ('m not)
	he she it	is.		he she it	is not. (isn't)
	you we they	are.		you we they	are not. (aren't)

Are you going** to be late? – **No, I'm not.
Is he going to** enjoy the trip? – **Yes, he is.
Are we going to** meet Mary? – **No, you aren't.

1 **Study the sentences in the box. Then fill in the blanks in the sentences below.**

> She is Australian
> Is she Australian? → Yes, she is.
>
> He's reading a book.
> Is he reading the paper? → No, he isn't.
>
> You're watching a movie.
> What movie are you watching?

a *She's* going to eat out. →
.... eat out? –
Yes, she ....

b *He's* going to see an exhibition. →
.... see a movie? – No, ...

c *You're* going to watch a movie. →
What movie .... ?

d *We're* going to meet at 6.00 →
What time .... meet?

2 **Make sentences with the correct form of *going to*.**

DANIEL: I / leave / university.
I'm going to leave university.
KATY: Why / do / that / ?
DANIEL: I / become / a singer in a band.
KATY: How / you / buy / food / ?
DANIEL: I / eat / at my parents' house.
KATY: Do your parents know?
DANIEL: No, they don't.
KATY: you / tell them / ?
DANIEL: Yes, of course.
KATY: When / you / tell them / ?
DANIEL: Soon.
KATY: they / be happy / for you / ?
DANIEL: Yes, because I / be / famous / !
KATY: Really? Hey, I play the guitar really well.

3 Fill in the blanks with the correct form of *going to* future of the verbs in brackets.

Do you love Cowden? Do you like green spaces?

Cowden Park is a beautiful green space. But it (**a**) ......is not...... (not be) green or beautiful any more. They (**b**) .... (cut) down the trees. They (**c**) .... (build) a shopping mall and a big car park.

We don't want a shopping mall. Our children (**d**) .... (not have) a safe place to play in. Cowden (**e**) .... (not have) enough green spaces. There (**f**) .... (be) more traffic and Cowden (**g**) .... (not be) a quiet village any more.

The building company says it's good for Cowden because we (**h**) .... (have) many good shops and many people (**i**) .... (get) jobs in the shops. We don't agree.

Come to the Town Hall on 25th July to give your opinion.

4 Write questions and answers about the advert.

a Cowden Park / always be green?
Is Cowden Park always going to be green? No, it isn't.

b the building company / keep the trees?
....? ....

c many people / work in the shopping mall?
....? ....

d people in Cowden / enjoy the shopping mall?
....? ....

e the children / play safely?
....? ....

f shoppers / have a place to park their cars?
....? ....

5 At the Town Hall. Ask the building company five questions. Use *going to*.

a plant new trees? ......Are you going to plant new trees?......

b car park free?...

c special area for children?...

d shopping mall open on Sundays? ....

e build shopping mall this year?...

6 **Read the leaflet. Answer the questions.**

a Which places are open now?
b Which places are going to open in the future?

Welcome to
The Melting Pot Arts Centre
Things are great at the Melting Pot and they're going to get better.

Cinema
Now open: Screens 1 and 2 for the best international cinema, old and new.
Coming in the autumn: *Bollywood Festival,* exciting films from India for all the family.

Food village
Food from around the world.
Two new restaurants opening soon:
Mamma Mia, food from the South of Italy.
Don't miss the ice cream week in October!
Chinatown, the best Cantonese food in town.
Special all-you-can-eat deal from 23 to 30 October (lunchtime only).

Concert Hall
Coming soon: Hot reggae band, *The Urban Rats* (September 15-17)
Dixiejazz, jazz from New Orleans (October 1-4).

The Circle Art Gallery:
The gallery is going to open in October with an exhibition of African Modern art, the best artists from the African continent.
In November, *People of the world in Britain,* a photography exhibition.

a Open now:
Screens 1 and 2
....
....

b Open in the future:
....
....
....

7 **Write questions and answers about future events at the arts centre using *is/are going to.***

a When / the Bollywood Festival / start?
When is the Bollywood Festival going to start?
....

b Who / play / at the Concert Hall / in October?
.... ?
....

c When / the reggae band / play?
.... ?
....

d What / special event / there / be / at *Mamma Mia*?
.... ?
....

e How long / the special deal at *Chinatown* / last?
.... ?
....

f How many / new places / open / at the Melting Pot?
.... ?
....

g What month / The Circle Art Gallery / open?
.... ?
....

h Where / the exhibition of African Art / be?
.... ?
....

UNIT 9

Imperatives

Affirmative	
Verb (base form)	
Stand up!	
Water	the plants twice a week.

Negative		
Auxiliary (*don't*)	**Verb (base form)**	
Don't	open	that door!
Don't	give	the cat too much water.

Use imperatives
– to give orders:
Sit down! Don't talk!

– to give instructions:
***Feed** the cat every day.*
***Don't forget** to open the window.*

1 Read this email and complete it with the correct verbs.

take give drink let (x2) feed

In

Delete Reply Reply All Forward Compose Mailboxes Get Mail Junk

From: Susie Jones
To: Jenny White
Cc:
Subject: Looking after Rusty

Dear Jenny,

Thanks for looking after Rusty when I go away. Here are a few things you need to know. You have to **(a)** ......take...... him for a walk every day and you must **(b)** .... him twice a day. He loves chocolate, but you mustn't **(c)** .... him chocolate. Rusty needs to **(d)** .... water in the mornings. When you arrive you can **(e)** .... him out in the garden, but you mustn't **(f)** .... him go on the street.

Thanks,
Susie

2 Now complete Jenny's notes.

a Take Rusty for a walk every day.
b .... him twice a day.
c Don't give .... chocolate.
d .... Rusty water in the morning.
e .... Rusty go out in the garden.
f .... him go on the street.

3 Now look at these notes and complete them with a verb in the affirmative or the negative.

feed	give	forget	leave

a Don't forget to take your keys.
b .... the doors open.
c .... the dog in the evening.
d .... the rabbit some salad.
e .... sugar to the dog.
f .... the windows closed.

4 Read these instructions for looking after aquarium fish. Change the instructions using imperatives.

The first thing to remember is that you must buy a fish tank that is not too big and not too small.

a Buy a fish tank that is not too big or too small.

You must give the fish enough water.

b ....

You must change the water every week and you have to be careful to keep the water clean.

c ....

Make sure that you do not put anything in the water.

d ....

Fish need to have plants in the water to provide shelter.

e ....

The aquarium must not be in direct sunlight, because this is too hot for the fish.

f ....

You must feed the fish every day, but be careful not to give the fish too much food.

g ....

5 Write sentences using imperatives.

a Don't park here.

b ....

c ....

d ....

e ....

f ....

g ....

h ....

6 **Are these sentences orders or instructions? Write O or I. (Look at page 29 again.)**

a Don't forget! ...O...

b Make sure you have lots of fresh water for your dog. ....

c Sit! ....

d Give your dog food! ....

e Read these tips. ....

f Take your dog for a walk often. ....

g Come! ....

7 **Now write the sentences from Activity 6 in the correct place in the text.**

So, you've got a new puppy! Remember, dogs must behave well.

(a) ...Read these tips...

-  Dogs need lots of exercise. (b) .... But puppies like to run and play with other dogs. Sometimes, they don't come back when you call them. Say "(c) ...." and clap your hands when your puppy comes back.
-  (d) .... Feed him twice a day. (e) ....  They drink very often.
- Dogs mustn't jump up on people. If your puppy jumps up, tell him, "(f) ...." (g) .... - your dog can be your best friend!

8 **You are going away for a few days. Write some instructions for a friend who is going to look after your flat / pet / garden / car. (Choose one.)**

....

....

....

....

....

UNIT 10

must, have to

Must

Affirmative		
I You He/She/It We They	must	be on time.

Negative		
I You He/She/It We They	must not (mustn't)	be late.

Interrogative		
Must	I you he/she/it we they	take this medicine?

Short answers					
Affirmative			Negative		
Yes,	I you he/she/it we they	must.	No,	I you he/she/it we they	mustn't.

Use *must* to talk about something which it is very important to do (obligation):

DOCTOR: *You **must** stay in bed.*

Use *mustn't* to talk about something which it is very important not to do (prohibition):

DOCTOR: *You **mustn't** go outside.*

Have to

Affirmative		
I You We They	have to	wash the car.
He/She/It	has to	

Negative		
I You We They	don't have to	go to class tomorrow.
He/She/It	doesn't have to	

Interrogative		
Do	I you we they	have to write emails?
Does	he/she/it	

Short answers					
Affirmative			Negative		
Yes,	I you we they	do.	No,	I you we they	don't.
	he/she/it	does.		he/she/it	doesn't.

Use *have to* to talk about something which it is important to do (obligation):

TEACHER: *You **have to** do your homework.*

Use *don't have to* to talk about something which is not important, something you have no obligation to do:

TEACHER: *You **don't have to** sit in the same seats every day.*

1 Look at these rules and write them in the correct column.

Rules for Art class
You **must** clean up after class.
You **mustn't** eat during class.
You **don't have to** be silent during class.
You **don't have to** stay in your seat.
You **mustn't** touch other people's work.
You **mustn't** work on other subjects during art class.
You **mustn't** run in the art classroom.
You **must** stay until the bell rings.
You **must** ask for permission to leave the classroom.

Yes	No	Not necessary
clean up after class		

2 Now complete these questions and answer them.

a Do .... you have to clean up after class?
....

b Do .... stay in your seat?
....

c .... stay until the bell rings?
....

d .... ask permission to leave the classroom? ....

e .... be silent during class?
....

3 Find the mistakes in these sentences and correct them below.

a You must ~~to~~ study hard.
You must study hard.

b We don't has to go to every class.
....

c They haven't to do any homework.
....

d Do you must speak French at work?
....

e Can you borrow me some money?
....

f Can I lend your MP3 player?
....

4 Read Joe's notices and complete the sentences.

a Joe ...has to... wear smart clothes to the party.

b He .... wear a tie.

c Joe .... remember to phone Sally at 3 p.m.

d The drama rehearsal .... start at 7.30 p.m, because it .... finish by 10 p.m.

e Joe and the other actors .... be late.

f To do the Cycling Tour of Paris, all cyclists .... wear helmets.

g They .... have maps.

h Joe .... forget Gloria's birthday.

i If you want to enter the competition, you .... post your entry by 31st March.

j Joe .... go shopping soon, for coffee, sugar and cereal.

UNIT 11

The past simple of verb *be*

Affirmative	
I was You were He was She was It was We were You were They were	at home yesterday.

Negative	
I was not (wasn't) You were not (weren't) He/She/It was not (wasn't) We were not (weren't) You were not (weren't) They were not (weren't)	at school yesterday.

Interrogative		Short answers			
		Affirmative		Negative	
Was I Were you Was he/she/it Were we Were you Were they	at the party?	Yes,	I was. you were. he/she/it was. we were. you were they were.	No,	I wasn't. you weren't. he/she/it wasn't. we weren't. you weren't. they weren't.

Use the past simple of *be* to describe a situation in the past:

Was Kevin at school yesterday? – No, he ***was*** *at a party.*

You normally use contractions in the negative:

Were *your parents at home on Saturday? – No, they* ***weren't****.*

1 **Louise is on the phone, talking to her boyfriend Kevin. Which sentences refer to the past and which ones to the present? Write *past* or *present*.**

KEVIN: Hi Louise! There you are! Where were you this morning? (**a**) ....past....

LOUISE: I wasn't at work. (**b**) .... I was at the shopping centre. (**c**) .... The stars from the TV show *Young Love* were there. (**d**) ....

KEVIN: That's great! Where are you now? (**e**) ....

LOUISE: I'm at work. (**f**) .... My boss wasn't here this morning, (**g**) .... but now she's here! (**h**) .... Bye!

2 **Complete this conversation with the past or present of *be*.**

a Hi Lyndsay! ....Are.... you working at the moment?

b Hi Paul! No, I .... at home watching TV. What about you?

c I .... with my brother. We .... at the club.

d Oh really? I .... at the club yesterday with my friend, Julie.

e .... you there all day?

f No, we .... there in the morning but we .... there in the afternoon.

g .... there a lot of people there now?

h No, there .... many people here. Come over!

i OK. See you soon.

3 Look at this table. Write questions for these answers.

	Last week	Yesterday	Today
Kim	in London	in France	at home
Laura and John	in Athens	at John's house	at Laura's house

a .... ? In France.

b .... ? At John's house.

c .... ? At Laura's house.

d .... ? In London.

e .... ? In Athens.

f .... ? At home.

4 Complete the dialogue with the past simple of *be*.

KEIRA: Hi, Jackie! It's Keira – in South Africa!

JACKIE: Where are you?

KEIRA: I'm in a little place called Arniston.

JACKIE: But you (**a**) ...were... in Durban last week!

KEIRA: Yes, for a week. My whole family (**b**) .... there!

JACKIE: (**c**) .... it a special occasion?

KEIRA: It (**d**) .... my cousin's twenty-first birthday. There (**e**) .... a huge party for her. And there (**f**) .... Zulu dancers! I love African dancing …

JACKIE: What (**g**) .... the weather like in Durban?

KEIRA: Hot! We (**h**) .... on the beach every day. There (**i**) .... any rain at all.

JACKIE: Send me an email and tell me all about Arniston!

KEIRA: Bye!

5 Now complete Keira's postcard.

Dear Jackie

At last – we're in beautiful Cape Town! Yesterday I (a) ...was... in a little place called Arniston. Our friends the Scotts (b) .... there on holiday. The beach (c) .... amazing – there (d) .... huge waves for surfing. It (e) .... crowded either, becaus the schools here (f) .... closed for the summer holidays. In fact, we (g) .... the only people on the beach!

This morning, while you (h) .... at work, I (i) .... on top of Tabl Mountain. Don't you wish you (j) .... here too!

I'll try to call you later this week. I hope your exams (k) .... too hard!

Love

Keira

6 Read the dialogues. Match the dialogue to the picture.

a

b

Conversation 1 Picture ....

MINA: Hi John!
JOHN: Hi Mina!
MINA: Where are you?
JOHN: We're at home.
MINA: Where were you this afternoon?
JOHN: We were at the zoo.
MINA: Oh.

Conversation 2 Picture ....

FRED: Hi Louise!
LOUISE: Hello Fred.
FRED: Where are you?
LOUISE: I'm at the zoo with Matt.
FRED: Where were you this morning?
LOUISE: At home. Why?

Answer these questions.

a Where is John now? ...At home...
b Where are Louise and Matt now? ....
c Was John at home in the afternoon? ....
d Were Matt and Louise at the zoo in the morning? ....

7 Look at the pictures and complete these questions and answers about Louise's day.

a Where ...was... Louise this morning at 8.00 am? She .... in bed.
b .... Louise in the gym at 7.00 pm? Yes, ...
c .... Louise and Frankie at the office at lunchtime? No, ... They ....
d .... ? She .... in the office.
e Where .... now? She .... at home.
f What .... ? She ....

UNIT 12

The past simple: affirmative, negative

Affirmative		
	Verb (base form + *-ed*)	
I You He/She/It We They	watched	a good film last night.

Negative			
	Auxiliary verb (*did + not*)	Verb (base form)	
I You He/She/It We They	did not (didn't)	watch	a good film last night.

To form the past simple, add *-ed* to the base form of the verb:
*watch – **watched***

Note some spelling irregularities:
*live – **lived***
*study – **studied***

Some irregular verbs in the past simple tense do not have *-ed* endings:

*be – **was***	*go – **went***
*become – **became***	*have – **had***
*break – **broke***	*leave – **left***
*die – **died***	*read – **read***
*do – **did***	*see – **saw***
*find – **found***	*take – **took***
*give – **gave***	*write – **wrote***

Use the past simple to talk about completed actions in the past:
*We **watched** a good film last night.*
*I **read** a good book two days ago.*
*I **saw** my old friend Kate the other day.*

1 Match the verbs with their past simple forms. Then complete the sentences *a–f* with verbs in the past simple.

Base form	Past simple form
break	lived
die	died
do	wrote
give	studied
go	wanted
have	worked
like	liked
live	saw
read	watched
see	broke
study	read
want	went
watch	did
work	gave
write	had

a We studied (study) World History at school.

b We .... (watch) a film about the First World War. Millions of soldiers .... (die).

c Louis XVI .... (live) in Versailles, near Paris.

d My mother .... (work) at the History Museum for 10 years.

e I .... (read) a book about the French Revolution. I .... (like) it very much.

f Marco Polo was a great traveller. He .... (go) to many countries and .... (see) many interesting things. He .... (write) about his trips.

2 Read the sentences and label the pictures *Daisy*, *Lily* and *Poppy*.

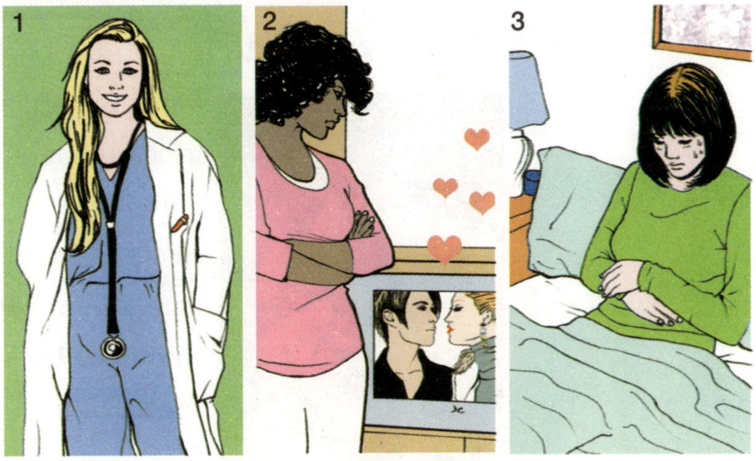

....

a She didn't watch Love Story last night.
Daisy didn't watch Love Story last night.

b She didn't sleep in her bed last night.
....

c Daisy always hated romantic things.
....

d She felt sick all morning.
....

e Poppy ate too much last night. Now she is sick in bed. ....

f She didn't go home last night.
....

g She didn't want to eat anything this morning.
....

h She didn't listen to *Romance* on the radio.
....

i Lily worked all night at the hospital. She can sleep all day. ....

Rewrite the sentences, replacing the word *she* with the names of the women.

3 Change the parts underlined to write about your weekend, a nice weekend.

<u>I didn't go to a party</u> on Saturday. I <u>didn't talk on the phone</u> all day and I <u>didn't go to bed late</u>.
<u>I didn't get bored</u> on Sunday. <u>I didn't watch television</u> all day and <u>I didn't eat any cake</u>.
It was a strange, but nice weekend!

....
....
....
....

4 Fill in the blanks in the biography with the past simple form of the verbs in brackets. Look at the list of irregular verbs on page 38 for help.

Gama, Vasco da Born 1460 in Portugal. Died 1524.

Vasco da Gama (a) ...was... (*be* irreg.) the first European to go to India by sea.

He (b) .... (*leave* irreg.) Portugal in 1497 with four small ships and 170 men. He sailed into the Atlantic and (c) .... (*turn* reg.) east to go round the Cape of Good Hope, at the tip of Africa. It (d) .... (*not be* irreg.) easy but Da Gama (e) .... (*continue* irreg.) on his voyage. After three months, the Portuguese reached the coast north of the Cape and sailed along the coast. They (f) .... (*find* irreg.) Arab towns on the coast of what is now Mozambique. Da Gama (g) .... (*become* irreg.) a friend of the Sultan of Malindi. The Sultan (h) .... (*give* irreg.) him two Arab pilots to guide him to India. Da Gama sailed across the Indian Ocean to Calicut. There, he (i) .... (*start* reg.) to trade with the ruler, Zamorin. In 1501, he (j) .... (*arrive* reg.) back in Portugal with ships full of spices.

Da Gama (k) .... (*become* irreg.) viceroy of India in 1524. He (l) .... (*die* reg.) in India on 24th December that year.

5 These sentences are all false. Rewrite them to make them true.

a Vasco da Gama left Portugal in 1597.
He didn't leave in 1597. He left in 1497.

b He took 200 men with him.
....

c He turned west to go round the Cape of Good Hope. ....

d He reached the coast north of the Cape after three years. ....

e The Sultan of Malindi gave him two Arab ships to go to India.
....

f Vasco da Gama died in Portugal.
....

Possession, prepositions

Possession: Use apostrophe *s* (*'s*) after a name to indicate possession:

That's John's jacket. (That jacket belongs to John.)
This is Mary's brother. (Mary has got a brother.)

Note that *'s* can also be
– the abbreviation of *is*:
John's watching TV. = John ***is*** *watching TV.*
– the abbreviation of *has*:
She's got green eyes. – She ***has*** *got green eyes.*

Prepositions: Use these prepositions to describe location (the place where something is):

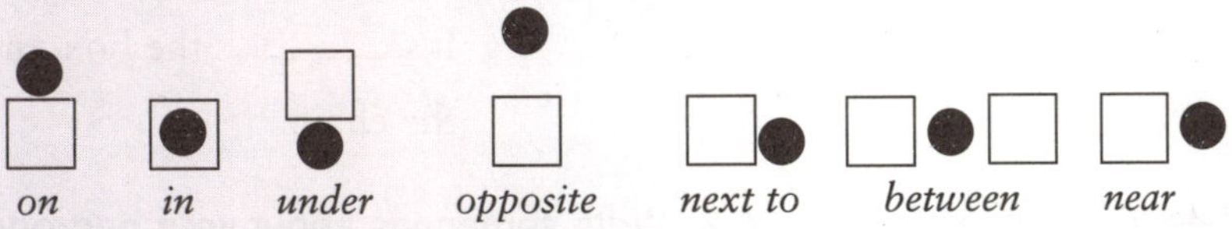

The cat is ***under*** *the car.*
The bank is ***next to*** *the bookstore.*
The restaurant is ***opposite*** *the supermarket.*

1 **Look at the Brown family's calendar and complete the sentences.**

FEBRUARY	1	2 Birthday: Daisy	3	4	5 Birthday: Grandma	6	7	8	9
	10	11 Pauline- music exam	12	13	14 Dad- Golf tournament	15	16 Birthday: Mum	17	18 Dog to the vet today: 2 p.m.
19	20 School cake sale	21	22 Birthday: Peter	23	24 Mum & Dad: Wedding anniversary	25	26	27 Drama performance: Daisy	28

a 2 February: It's Daisy's birthday
b 5 February: .... birthday
c 22 February: .... birthday
d 11 February: .... music exam
e 16 February: .... birthday
f 14 February: .... golf tournament
g 18 February: .... vet appointment
h 27 February: .... drama performance
i 24 February: .... wedding anniversary

2 Look at these pictures.

between	in	near	next to	on	opposite	under

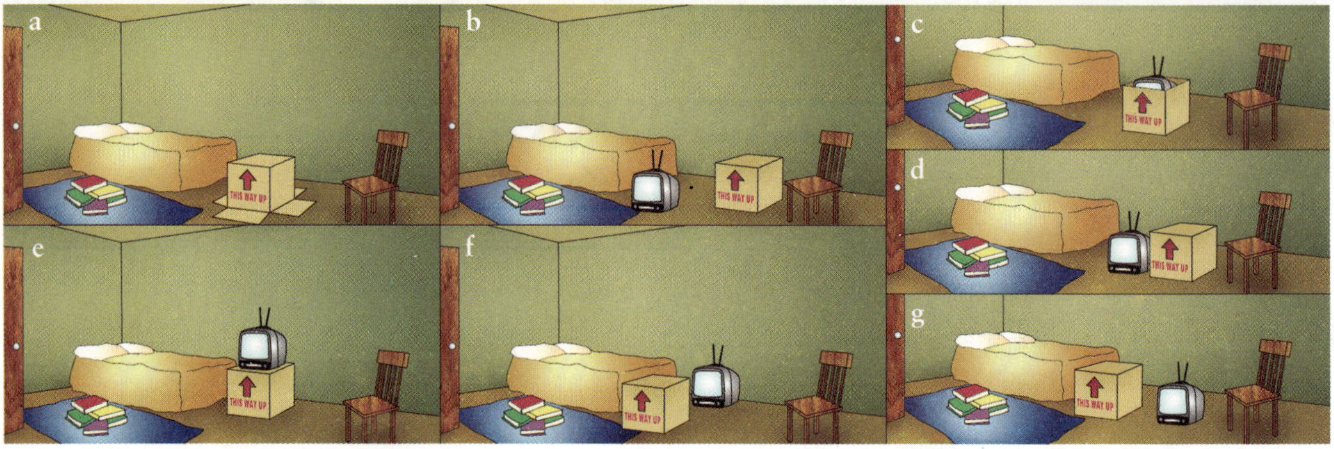

Where is the TV? Write the correct preposition.

a It's ....under.... the box.
b It's .... the box.
c It's .... the box.
d It's .... the box.
e It's .... the box.
f It's .... the box.
g It's .... the box and the chair.

3 Look at the picture and complete the sentences about Jane and Martin's possessions.

a Jane's shoes are ....under the bed.... .
b .... next to the desk.
c .... is opposite the door.
d Martin's book ....
e Jane's lamp is .... the bed and ....
f Martin's .... on ....
g Martin and Jane's computer .... near ....

4 Write sentences about your bedroom.

Where is the

a bed
b wardrobe
c desk/table
d chair
e window
f door

The bed is under the window.
....
....
....
....
....

5 Read these two sentences.

a Melanie's five years old.
b Melanie's parents are in the shopping centre.

Which of the sentences contains

1 a possessive *'s*?
2 a short form of the verb *be* (*Melanie is* ...)?

6 What is the meaning of *'s* in the sentences *a–d*? Write P (possession) or *Be* (abbreviation of *is*).

a Scott's five friends ......P......
b Jenny's teacher ....
c Jenny's a teacher ....
d Scott's five ....

Write *a–d* as captions under the pictures.

1 ....

2 ....

3 ....

4 ....

7 Find the mistakes in these sentences and correct them below.

a What's his wife's name? Her name's ~~is~~ Jane.
What's his wife's name? her name's Jane.

b How old is your daughter? My daughter's is 20.
....

c What does your son do? He's student.
....

d What colour is Jimmy's car? He's car blue.
....

e Is James a doctor? No, he's is a dentist.
....

f What's your brother name? His name Rafael.
....

8 Complete the sentences about Rory's family.

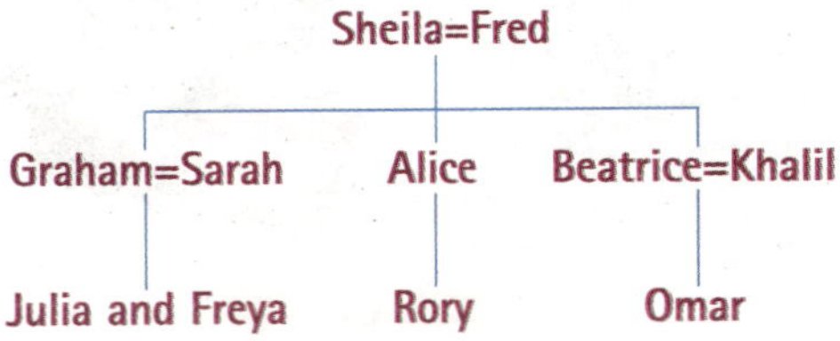

a Sheila's Rory's grandmother .
b Rory's .... called Fred.
c Alice and Beatrice are .... sisters.
d Rory's .... son.
e Rory, Julia and Freya are .... cousins.
f Sarah's .... wife.
g Khalil's .... husband.
h Julia's .... sister.

Now write similar sentences about your family.

....
....
....
....
....
....
....
....

UNIT 14

Possessive adjectives

My Your His Her Our Their Its	job is interesting. friends are American. colour is grey.

Maria's from Spain. **Her** *friends are Spanish.*
Julio's from Mexico. **His** *friends are Mexican.*
The dog's *Pongo.* **Its** *name is Pongo.*

1 Complete the questions with *my*, *your*, *his*, *her*, *our* or *their*.

a

What's .... job?

b

What's .... job?

c

What's .... job?

d

What's .... job?

e

f

g

What's .... job?

h

i

What's .... job?

j

2 Now find and complete the answers to the questions in Activity 1.

1 We're students! ...Our... favourite subject is History. [e]

2 He's a bus driver. .... bus is number 19. [ ]

3 I'm a student. .... book is called *Just Skills*. [ ]

4 She's an engineer. .... job is building bridges and offices. [ ]

5 They are bakers. They sell .... bread in supermarkets. [ ]

6 I'm an artist. You can see the paint on .... clothes! [ ]

7 They're dancers. .... dancing is great. [ ]

8 We're nurses. We think .... job is very important. [ ]

9 He's an accountant. .... Maths is very good. [ ]

10 She's a doctor. .... job is in a children's hospital. [ ]

3 Circle the correct word.

A

A: Do (**a**) *you* / *your* know the man over there?

B: The man with a drink in (**b**) *his* / *her* hand? Yes, that's Mark Lake. (**c**) *He's* / *His* a teacher. (**d**) *My* / *Their* children really like him – he's (**e**) *your* / *their* favourite! And that's (**f**) *her* / *his* wife next to him.

B

JOHN: I really like (**g**) *your* / *you* ideas, Charles. We want someone to design (**h**) *her* / *our* new catalogue. Why don't (**i**) *you* / *your* come to (**j**) *my* / *her* office with me? Then you can meet my boss. (**k**) *His* / *Her* name's Catherine Hughes.

C

A: Are those (**l**) *your* / *our* new earrings? (**m**) *They're* / *Their* very nice.

B: Thanks. (**n**) *They* / *Their* were a present from my boyfriend, for (**o**) *my* / *her* birthday.

4 Match the sentence pairs.

a That's my cousin Isabella.	[5]	**1** It's my favourite.
b Alexander is a teacher.	[ ]	**2** Our house is in Dean St.
c We are new here.	[ ]	**3** Your taxi is here.
d Meet Sam and Alison.	[ ]	**4** This is his first job.
e Are you Mr Brent?	[ ]	**5** Her mother is my father's sister.
f I love this song.	[ ]	**6** They're from Chicago.

5 Fill in the blanks with a possessive adjective (*my*, *your*, *his*, *her*, *its*, *our*, *their*).

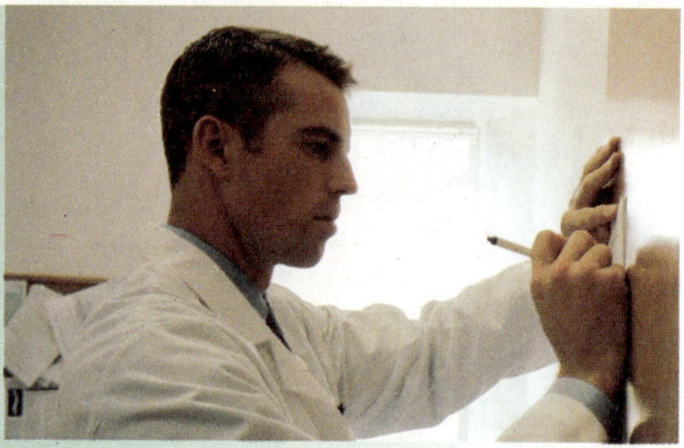

Rachel, Thomas and I are friends. We work in hospital. I'm a doctor. (a) ...My... job is interesting. Rachel and Thomas are nurses. (b) .... job is interesting too. (c) .... hospital is very big. (d) .... name is Stafford Memorial Hospital. Rachel is a good cook but it isn't her job; it's (e) .... hobby. Thomas is a good singer. (f) .... songs are nice. What's (g) .... job?

6 Circle the correct words in the sentences.

a *They're* / *Their* job is interesting.
They're / *Their* engineers.
b This is Kuba. *It's* / *Its* a nice cat.
This is my cat. *It's* / *Its* name is Kuba.
c *You're* / *Your* a teacher.
You're / *Your* teacher is South African.
d *He's* / *His* a baker.
He's / *His* job is difficult.
e *They're* / *Their* Sooty and Lucy, my cats.
My cats are sleeping in *their* / *they're* basket.
f Do you remember Oliver? *He's* / *His* my nephew.
His / *He's* father is an actor.
g I work in a shop. *Its* / *It's* in the High Street.
It's / *Its* owner is from Poland.
h *Your* / *You're* doing very well.
Did anyone help you with *you're* / *your* homework?
i Mark isn't Linda's husband; *he's* / *his* her boyfriend.
His / *He's* new car is a Porsche.
j My cousins live in Canada – *they're* / *their* father is Canadian, you see.
They're / *Their* at High School in Vancouver.

7 Rewrite the words in brackets. Use possessive adjectives instead.

a That's Guzide. (Guzide's) .... home language is Turkish.
That's Guzide. Her home language is Turkish.

b My brother works in an office. (My brother's) .... office is in the centre of the city.

c I work for a big company. (The company's) .... offices are in Brussels.

d I'm on holiday with my family. We've got a holiday house here. That's (my family's) .... house over there.

e Jasmine and Liam are going to Brazil for (Jasmine and Liam's) .... holiday.

f These are my friends Christina and Ana, from English class. We're shopping for (the English class's) .... party on Saturday.

g Do you teach at this school? My sister goes to this school.
Really? What's (your sister's) .... name?

h The children love football. (The children's) .... favourite team is Arsenal.

UNIT 15

The present simple: affirmative, negative

Affirmative		
I You We They	go to work get up	at 8 o'clock.
He/She/It	goes gets up	

Negative			
I You We They	do not (don't)	go to work get up	at 8 o'clock.
He/She/It	does not (doesn't)		

After *he/she/it*, add *-s* to the verb:
She drives a bus.

Note these different spellings.
Verb *go*:
*He **goes** to bed.*

Verbs ending in consonant + *-y*, such as *study*:
*She **studies** English.*

Verb *have*:
*Helen **has** breakfast at 8 o'clock.*

Use the present simple
– to talk about regular and habitual actions:
*I **get up** at 6 o'clock.*

– to talk about facts that are permanent:
*He **works** in a hospital.*

1 Fill in the blanks with the correct present simple form of the verbs in brackets.

Many people in Britain (**a**) read.......... (read) the paper in the morning, at breakfast or on the bus or train. Milan and Neela Joshi are newsagents. They sell newspapers and magazines. Neela (**b**) .... (get up) at 5.00. She (**c**) .... (have) a shower but she (**d**) .... (not have) breakfast. She takes the papers to lots of houses at 6.30 every morning, Sundays too.

Milan (**e**) .... (get up) at 6.30 and (**f**) .... (open) the shop at 8.00. They (**g**) .... (close) the shop at 9.00 p.m. In the evening they (**h**) .... (relax). Milan (**i**) .... (watch) television and Neela (**j**) .... (read) the papers! They (**k**) .... (not see) their friends in the week, only on Sunday afternoon. 'We work very hard,' says Neela, 'but we like our job!'

2 True or false?

a Many people in Britain read the paper in the evening. T F
b Neela reads the papers in the morning. T F
c Milan works in the shop. T F
d He opens the shop at 7.00. T F
e The Joshis work from 6.00 a.m. to 8.00 p.m. T F
f They work on Sunday afternoon too. T F
g Neela has breakfast after her shower. T F

3 Read the sentences and label the people in the pictures.

a Rick works in a hospital.

b Clara drives a bus.

c Martin and Karen are students. They don't work very hard.

d Karen studies architecture in the morning and relaxes in the afternoon.

e Paul works on a plane but he doesn't fly it.

f Martin goes to the same classes as Karen, and watches TV in the afternoon.

g Lily plays the piano in a theatre.

4 Complete the sentences with the present simple form of the verbs in brackets.

a Rick ...works... (work) all night. He .... (sleep) all day.

b All the people in the pictures .... (live) in the same house.

c Martin and Karen .... (not work) very hard.

d Lily .... (not dance) at the theatre. She .... (play) the piano.

e Clara .... (like) her job but she .... (study) Spanish in the evenings.

f Martin and Karen .... (not go) to university in the afternoon.

g Paul .... (not see) his friends every day.

5 Write true sentences.

Example: I don't sleep all day.

I My friend and I My parents	(don't)	work(s) in an office play(s) the piano read(s) the paper have/has a shower watch(es) television sleep(s) study/studies	every day. in the morning. in the evening. all day. all night.
My brother My sister	(doesn't)		

....

....

....

....

6 Read the survey. Complete the sentences.

This is your life!

We want to find out how people live in our city. Please complete our survey!

Please tell us ...	**Name** Jim McLean	**Name** Lucy Morris	**YOU**
about the transport you use	I go to work by bike. I don't drive a car.	I take a bus to work.	
what you have for lunch at work	I buy a sandwich from a shop near my office.	I have lunch at the office.	
your opinion of fast food	I eat fast food (but not every day)!	I don't eat fast food – I hate it.	
the sports and exercise you do – tennis? swimming? yoga?	I play tennis. I don't go swimming. I ski every winter, in Austria. I don't do yoga.	I play tennis. I don't go swimming. I ski every winter, in France. I do yoga every week.	
the music you like	I love rock music. I don't listen to anything else.	I don't like rock music. I enjoy classical music.	

a Jim and Lucy ...play... tennis, but they ...don't go... swimming.

b Jim .... yoga, but Lucy .... it every week.

c Jim .... fast food but he .... it every day.

d Lucy .... fast food. She .... it.

e Jim .... rock music. He .... to anything else.

f Lucy .... rock music. She .... classical music.

g Jim and Lucy .... every winter.

h Jim .... to Austria, and Lucy .... to France.

i Jim .... drive to work. He .... to work by bike.

j Lucy .... the bus to work.

k Lucy .... lunch at the office. Jim .... a sandwich from a shop near his office.

7 Write sentences that are true for you in the last column.

8 Write true sentences about you and your family and friends. Write

- how you travel to college or work

 ....

- what you have for lunch

 For lunch, I have a salad from the canteen. Or I make a sandwich at home ...

 ....

- where your best friend works or studies

 ....

- where your parents live

 ....

- what you and your friends do at the weekends

 ....

The present simple: *yes/no* questions and short answers

Interrogative			
Do	I you we they	have a shower	every day?
Does	he/she/it		

Short answers					
Affirmative			Negative		
Yes,	I you we they	do.	No,	I you we they	don't.
	he/she/it	does.		he/she/it	doesn't.

For short answers to questions containing a form of *do*, re-use the same form:

Does your sister study architecture? – **Yes,** *she* **does.**

Do your parents watch television in the afternoon? – **No,** *they* **don't.**

Yes/No questions have rising intonation at the end:

Do you like cooking?

1 Read the questions in the food questionnaire. Then complete the information in *a–c* below.

a Number of verbs in each question: ...2... .

b Questions 1 – 5, first verb: .... ;
second verb: ....

c Questions 6 – 7 : first verb: .... ;
second verb: ....

What do your eating habits say about you?

Answer the questionnaire and find out!

1 Do you have snacks between meals?
2 Do you eat breakfast?
3 Do you like vegetables?
4 Do you drink tea and coffee?
5 Do you eat fish at least once a week?
6 Does your family have meals together at least once a day?
7 Does your family watch TV during meals?

2 Answer the questions in the questionnaire for yourself.

1 Do you have snacks between meals?
Yes, I do/No, I don't.

3 Complete the questions with the verbs in brackets. Write answers.

a ...Do... you ...like... (like) fish? –
...Yes, I do/No, I don't.......

b .... you .... (like) cooking?

c .... your brothers and sisters .... (buy) snacks?

d .... your father .... (like) his job?

e .... your partner .... (drink) milk?

f .... your partner .... (eat) fish?

g .... the people in your class .... (work) hard?

h .... your partner .... (have) good eating habits?

4 Read the information. Write the names of the people.

This person:

a doesn't eat meat, red or white. ......Raj......

b eats meat every day. ....

c drinks tea. ....

d eats bread at lunch. ....

e has soup for breakfast. ....

f eats vegetables at the three meals. ....

g likes crisps. ....

Maiko (Japan) Breakfast: soup, rice and egg or fish. Lunch and dinner: fish or chicken only (one day a week), rice, vegetables and fruit. Drink: Green tea, soda

Sandy (USA) Breakfast: milk, bread and eggs. Lunch: hamburger or sandwich, crisps. Dinner: meat or chicken with vegetables. Drink: coffee, soda

Raj (India) Breakfast: rice, vegetables, pulses (e.g. beans and lentils), fruit. Lunch and dinner: vegetables in different sauces, different kinds of bread and pulses. Drink: yoghurt drink, water

5 Write questions and answers about the people in Activity 4.

a Maiko / meat?

...Does Maiko eat meat...? ...Yes, she does... .

b Sandy / fish?

.......................? ....

c Maiko and Raj / fruit?

.......................? ....

d Maiko / bread?

.......................? ....

e Maiko / Raj / a lot of rice?

.......................? ....

6 Reorder the words to write questions.

a Do / eat / people in this country / for breakfast / eggs / ?

.... Yes, they do.

b they / Do / like / a lot of meat / to eat / ?

.... No, they don't.

c a lot of coffee / drink / Do / they / ?

.... No, they don't.

d have / a lot of / fish / Do / they / ?

.... Yes, they do.

e like / they / rice / Do / ?

.... Yes, they do.

Which country are the questions about?

....

7 Complete the questions with the correct form of *be* or *do*.

Write answers that are true for you.

Are you single?

(a) .... you want to meet someone special?

(b) .... your friends try to match you with other single friends?

(c) .... you tired of meeting people who (d) .... not similar to you?

Then try our website!

We (e) .... here to help you!

f ....Are.... you older than 21? ....

g .... you drive a car? ....

h .... you live in a town or a city? ....

i .... your hair blonde? ....

j .... you good at sports? ....

k .... you like reggae music? ....

l .... you interested in fashion? ....

m .... you want to travel in your job? ....

n .... you like going to the cinema? ....

o .... your best friend in your class? ....

p .... anyone in your family live in another country? ....

q .... you play a musical instrument? ....

r .... your birthday in the first six months of the year? ....

s .... you like learning English? ....

8 You want to find a new friend. Write some questions with *be* or *have*.

....

....

....

....

UNIT 17

The present simple: *wh-/how* questions

To ask a question, you can use a question word:

Question word	Asks about:
What	a thing
Where	a place
Who	a person
Why	a reason
How	the manner

To ask a question with a question word, follow this pattern:

Question word	Auxiliary verb (*do/does*)	Subject	Verb (base form)
Where	do	you	live ?

Examples:

Question word	Auxiliary verb (*do/does*)	Subject (noun or pronoun)	Verb (base form)	
Why	do	I	live	in London?
Who	do	you	play	tennis with?
What	does	John	do	in his free time?
How	does	she	go	shopping?
Where	does	your dog	sleep?	
What	do	we	want	to do now?
Why	do	they	like	watching TV?

Wh-/How questions have falling intonation at the end:
When do you go to the cinema? ↘

1 Jack Nolan is a famous actor. Read the interviewer's questions *a–d* and match the questions with the answers *1–4*.

a What **do** you **do** in your free time?
b When **do** you **play** golf?
c Where **do** you **play**?
d Who **do** you **play** with?

2 **Now make questions about Kelly, Jack Nolan's daughter.**

a what / Kelly / do / free time? [ ]
What does Kelly do in her free time?

b where / Kelly / sing? [ ]
....

c who / Kelly / sing / with? [ ]
....

d when / Kelly / sing? [ ]
....

1 She's in a band called 'The Happy People'.

2 She loves singing.

3 She usually sings in the house with her band. They sometimes play in a club.

4 All the time! She always sings in the mornings. She often sings in the evenings with her band.

Match the answers with the questions.

3 **Put these words in the right order to make questions and answers.**

a do / What / free / you / time / do / your / in / ?
What do you do in your free time?

go / movies / I / often / the / to / .
....

b go / with / Who / you / do / ?
....

usually / go / friend / with / I / my / .
....

c your / does / Where / swimming / brother / go / ?
....

sometimes / goes / He / to / club / the / .
....

d does / go / When / he / ?
....

always / goes / on / He / Saturdays / .
....

4 **Write the correct form of the verb *do* in these questions.**

a Where ...does... Cristina play soccer?

b When .... Billy and Ned go swimming?

c What .... Janie do in her free time?

d Who .... they go shopping with?

5 **Match the answers to the questions in Activity 4.**

1 They usually go on Tuesdays. [b]

2 Near her house. [ ]

3 Their parents. [ ]

4 She often watches TV. [ ]

6 Match the questions *a–h* and the answers *1–8*.

a Why don't you like watching the news on TV? [4]
b Who do you sit next to in class? [ ]
c Where do you usually go on holiday? [ ]
d What time do you get up on a Saturday? [ ]
e When do you check your emails? [ ]
f How many times a week do you eat meat? [ ]
g How do you get to work or school every day? [ ]
h What do you do to relax, at the weekend? [ ]

1 I read, or listen to music.
2 My friend, Miriam.
3 About three times.
4 Because it's boring.
5 Late – about 10 o'clock.
6 I go by bus.
7 To the seaside.
8 After breakfast, and before I go to bed.

7 Write questions for the underlined phrases.

a I play tennis with my friend, Beth.
Who do you play tennis with?

b We go to the disco on Friday nights.
....

c I always buy my clothes from Topshop.
....

d I walk to school, because it's healthy to walk!
....

e I ride a scooter.
....

f I visit friends, or we go out to restaurants, or to the cinema.
....

g It starts at 9.30 a.m.
....

h I wash my hair every day.
....

8 Look at the charts about weekly routines. Complete the questions, and write the answers in full sentences.

	Mon	Tues	Weds	Thurs	Fri	Sat	Sun
Linda	Work out		Work out		Work out		Lunch with parents
Patrick	Get up at 6.00	Get up at 6.00	Get up at 6.00	Get up at 6.00	Get up at 6.00	Get up at 9.00 Play soccer	Get up at 9.00
Sue and Jane	Watch TV	Watch TV	Watch TV	Watch TV	Go to the cinema	Go shopping	

a What does Linda do three times a week?
....

b .... a week .... Patrick play soccer?
....

c .... Sue and Jane do on Fridays?
....

d .... Linda have lunch with on Sundays?
....

e .... time .... Patrick get up on a Sunday?
....

f How .... Sue and Jane spend their Saturdays?
....

UNIT 18

The present continuous

Affirmative		
Subject	**Verb *be***	**Verb + *-ing***
I	am ('m)	having dinner.
You	are ('re)	
Marie and Sally John and I	are	
Susan He The dog	is ('s)	

***I'm having** dinner.*
***You're watching** TV.*
***John and I are going** for a walk.*

Negative				
Subject	**Verb *be***	***not***	**(contraction)**	**Verb + *-ing***
I	am	not	('m not)	having dinner.
You	are		('re not / aren't)	
Marie and Sally John and I	are		(aren't)	
Susan He The dog	is		('s not / isn't)	

***I'm not driving** this car.*
***You aren't taking** photos.*
*OR **You're not taking** photos.*
The dog's not running.
*OR **The dog isn't running.***

Yes/No questions		
Verb *be*	**Subject**	**Verb + *-ing***
Am	I	having dinner?
Are	you we they	
Is	he she it	

***Am I taking** the photos?*
***Is Luke dancing** with you?*
***Are we driving** home now?*

Use the present continuous to talk about actions happening at the moment of speaking, right now, or at present but over a period of time:

* **I'm not dancing – I'm having** dinner!*
* **He's living** in London with his parents.*

Note that if the verb ends in *-e*, the *-ing* form has no *e*:

* write → writing*

Short answers
Yes, I am. / No, I'm not.
Yes, you are. / No, you aren't.
Yes, he / she / it is. / No, he / she / it isn't.
Yes, we / they are. / No, we / they aren't.

1 **Write the correct form of the verb *be* in these sentences.**

a What ......is...... Jake doing?

b .... she singing?

c .... Susie and John going home?

d Where .... Lucy going?

e We .... watching TV.

f Maria .... not coming to the party.

g We .... not doing our homework right now.

h They .... listening to their new CD.

i I .... not working at the moment.

j What .... you doing right now, Jenny?

2 **Look at this picture and write what the people are doing.**

a ....

....

b ....

....

c ....

....

d ....

....

e ....

....

f ....

....

3 **Read the conversations and match them with the pictures, A, B, C or D.**

A

B

C

D

1 [A] [ ]

BEV: Pete? Where are you?

PETE: Hi, Bev. I'm driving home from work. Where are you?

BEV: At my house, with Jim and Becky. They're climbing the tree.

PETE: What? Why?

BEV: Just for fun. I'm taking photos. Come over.

PETE: No, I'm feeling really tired.

2 [ ] [ ]

ANGIE: Debbie, are you watching TV?

DEBBIE: Hi, Angie. No, I'm not. We're having dinner.

ANGIE: Well, Sam is on *Stars of Tomorrow*!

DEBBIE: Really? Is he dancing or what?

ANGIE: Yes, he is. Everyone is clapping and cheering!

4 **Complete the sentences with the correct part(s) of the present continuous.**

a Pete's ....driving........ (drive) home.

b Debbie isn't .... (watch) television. She .... (have) dinner.

c Becky and Jim .... (climb) the tree.

d .... they ....(watch) *Stars of Tomorrow*? – No, they aren't.

e Sam .... (dance) on television.

f Is Angie .... (watch) Sam? – Yes, she ....

g .... Bev .... (climb) the tree? – No, she ....

h Pete .... (not go) to Bev's house.

He .... (go) home.

i People like Sam's dance. They .... (cheer).

5 **Find six differences between the pictures. Use the affirmative and negative form of** ***be*** **to describe what the people are doing.**

A

B

a In Picture A, Tom is riding his bike. In Picture B, he isn't riding his bike. He's falling off his bike.

b ....

c ....

d ....

e ....

f ....

UNIT 19

The present continuous: *wh-* questions

Question word	Verb *be*	Subject	Verb + *-ing*
What Why Where	am	I	singing?
	are ('re)	you they we	
Who	is ('s)	she he it	singing with?

*What **am I doing** here?*
*Why **are you going** home?*
*Where **are they working** at the moment?*
*Who **is she living** with?*

1 Look at the picture and answer the questions.

a What is Heather doing?

She's walking on the catwalk.

b What is Nicole wearing?

....

c Who is Jed eating with?

....

d What is Chris wearing?

....

2 Look at the picture again and write the questions that go with these answers.

a Who is Marla eating with?

With Jed.

b ....?

A black dress and grey shoes.

c ....?

She's talking on her mobile phone.

d ....?

She's wearing a white T-shirt and black trousers and he's wearing a white T-shirt and jeans.

3 **Write questions. Use the pronouns and the present continuous of the verbs in brackets.**

a What ......is he studying...... (he/study)?

b What .... (you/eat)?

c Why .... (she/cry)?

d Where .... (you/phone) from?

e What .... (they/wear)?

f Who .... (you/have) lunch with?

4 **Match the questions in Activity 3 with the answers *1–6*.**

1 from the office d
2 my sister
3 uniforms
4 a salad
5 because her head hurts
6 English

5 **Complete the dialogues with the present continuous of the verbs in brackets.**

1

2

1

A: Don't turn around, but George Clooney is in the restaurant.

B: Really? Where (**a**) .... he .... (sit)?

A: Behind you.

B: What (**b**) .... he .... here? (do)

A: He (**c**) .... his dinner, of course! (have)

B: Who (**d**) .... he .... with? (eat) What (**e**) .... he ....? (wear)

A: He (**f**) .... with a young woman. (sit)

B: Oh, I really have to look. Dan! Don't be silly! That's not George Clooney at all!

2

A: Jack! Hi! What (**g**) .... you .... here? (do)

B: Hi, Sadia. I (**h**) .... photos of the models. (take) Why (**i**) .... you .... (stand) there?

A: Shh. I (**j**) .... a ticket for the show. (not got)

6 Sue is going out. Her mum has a lot of questions! Write the questions. Then answer them.

a MUM: (what / do?) What are you doing ?
SUE: I'm getting ready to go out.

b MUM: (where / go?) .... ?
SUE: ....

c MUM: (who / go / with?) .... ?
SUE: ....

d MUM: (where / meet?) .... ?
SUE: ....

e MUM: (how / get there?) .... ?
SUE: ....

f MUM: (what time / come back?) .... ?
SUE: ....

g MUM: (why / not wear / jeans?) .... ?
SUE: ....

7 Now write an email to a friend who is going out tonight. Ask questions.

Delete Reply Reply All Forward Compose Mailboxes Get Mail Junk

From:
To:

What are you doing tonight?

Where .... ?

Who .... ?

.... meet?

What time .... ?

Why .... ?

What .... wearing?

UNIT 20

The present continuous vs present simple

Present simple
Use the <u>present simple</u>
– to talk about habits and things you do regularly:
*I **get up** at five o'clock every day.*
*We **play** squash twice a week.*

– to give facts about people and things:
*Jane **lives** in France.*
*Water **boils** at 100°C.*

Present continuous
Use the <u>present continuous</u>
– to talk about things that are happening at this moment:
*What **are** you **doing**? – I'm **reading** a book.*

– to talk about things that are happening at this particular time:
***I'm working** in Paris for two months.*
*My brother **is living** in the USA for a year.*

1 Read the sentences. Underline the verbs. Label them PC (present continuous) or PS (present simple).

a She <u>works</u> for a magazine. PS
b She's working at home today.
c She's writing a new article.
d She writes articles about fashion.
e She has important meetings every day.
f She's making a phone call at the moment.

2 Match the sentences in Activity 1 with the meanings in the table. Label them PC or PS.

Meanings	Sentences	Present continuous or present simple?
1 habits, things we do regularly	e	
2 facts about things and people		
3 happening at this very moment, now, as we speak		
4 happening now (this week, this year, etc.)		

3 Complete these sentences with the present simple or present continuous tense.

a I usually work in an office, but today I 'm working (work) at home.
b At the moment I'm watching TV, but I never .... (watch) TV in the morning.
c Jake often writes emails, but today he .... (make) phone calls.
d Sally .... (not speak) French, but she .... (take) classes at the moment.
e Jack and Jenny .... (not take) photos very often, but today they're using their mobile phone to take pictures.
f Margarita .... (live) in Spain at the moment, but she usually .... (live) in Peru.

4 Write phrases from Activity 3 in the correct column.

Habits, things we do regularly	Facts about things and people	Happening at this very moment, now, as we speak	Happening now (this week, this year, etc.)
Jake often writes emails.			

5 Complete the sentences with the present continuous or the present simple of the verbs in brackets.

Ming usually (a) lives (live) in London but at the moment she (b) .... (live) in Hong Kong for a few months. She (c) .... (work) for a bank and she (d) .... (work) at the Hong Kong office. Ming's mother is Chinese so Ming (e) .... (speak) Chinese but she (f) .... (not speak) it very often, only to her mother. Ming is happy in Hong Kong. 'I (g) .... (speak) Chinese all the time now. And I (h) .... (meet) cousins for the first time. I (i) .... (learn) a lot about Chinese culture. It's my culture too. I (j) .... (have) fun!' says Ming.

6 Find the mistakes in these sentences and correct them.

a I always send reports ~~on~~ fax. I always send reports by fax.
b I'm usually living in London. ....
c She's never having important meetings. ....
d Do you want leave a message? ....
e Who's speaking? – I'm Joe. ....
f Can I taking a message? ....

7 Match the emails and the pictures.

A

Delete Reply Reply All Forward Compose Mailboxes Get Mail Junk »

Greetings from Montreal! We (a) .... (stay) at my aunt's flat. She (b) .... (not be) here – she (c) .... (work) in Toronto at the moment, because she (d) .... (be) a tour guide, and she (e) .... (travel) all over Canada. Everyone (f) .... (think) Canada is always cold, but right now, the sun (g) .... (shine) and I (h) .... (sit) here on the balcony, (i) .... (wear) just a T-shirt and shorts! The balcony (j) .... (be) above a busy square. Right now I (k) .... (watch) someone doing circus tricks. He's really good!

Love, Liz

1

2

3

B

Delete Reply Reply All Forward Compose Mailboxes Get Mail Junk

We're in Arizona. We (l) .... (ride) horses in the canyon. I (m) .... (love) it! We (n) .... (stay) on a ranch. There are lots of other activities as well – I (o) ....(learn) to abseil this week! Every morning we (p) .... (go) swimming. I (q) .... (practise) for a big tennis tournament on the ranch at the end of the week.

See you soon,
Joanna

C

Delete Reply Reply All Forward Compose Mailboxes Get Mail Junk

Guess where I am today? Here's a clue: I (r) .... (sit) on a beautiful beach. Every day I (s) .... (see) wonderful multi coloured fish under the water ... It's the Great Barrier Reef! I (t) .... (stay) at a campsite with some friends. We (u) .... (do) a scuba diving course here. I (v) .... (have) the most amazing holiday.

Alex

8 Complete the emails with the correct form of the verbs in brackets.

9 Find these phrases in the emails. Write sentences with these expressions about your life.

- a At the moment
- b Right now
- c This week
- d At the end of the week
- e Every day
- f Every morning
- g Today

At the moment, I'm reading a new book by Dan Brown.

....

....

....

....

....

....

UNIT 21

Subject pronouns and verb *be*

Affirmative			
Subject pronoun	**Verb *be***	**(Contraction)**	
I	am	(I'm)	
You	are	(You're)	
He	is	(He's)	
She	is	(She's)	here for the festival.
It	is	(It's)	
We	are	(We're)	
You	are	(You're)	
They	are	(They're)	

Use the present simple of *be* to describe the present situation:
***They're** my friends.*
***We're** in the same English class.*

You normally use contractions when you speak:
***I'm** Maria.*
***My name's** Peter.*

1 Match the phrases. Write them in the spaces.

a I am .... I'm ....
b ....
c ....
d ....
e ....
f ....
g ....
h ....

I am	my name is	he's	they are	we are
he is	you are	we're	my name's	I'm
they're	it's	she's	you're	it is	she is

2 It is the first day of the English class. Write the subject pronoun, *I*, *you*, *he*, *she*, *we* or *they*.

3 Fill in the blanks with *am*, *is* and *are*.

4 Complete the questions and answers for yourself.

a Who are you? – I'm.. .

b What' .... your name? – My name' ....

c Who' .... your teacher? – His/Her name' ....

d Who are your friends? – They'.............................. .... and ....

5 **Fill in the blanks with a form of the verb *be* (contracted if possible), your name and the names of two friends.**

NOAH: Hi! I (**a**) 'm........ Noah. What (**b**) .... your name?

YOU: My name (**c**) .... (*your name*) .... This (**d**) .... (*the name of a friend*) .... and this (**e**) .... (*the name of a friend*) .... They (**f**) .... my friends. We (**g**) .... in the same English class.

NOAH: Nice to meet you!

6 **Complete the sentences.**

I' (**a**) .... Carole. This (**b**) .... Yusef and this (**c**) .... Nadia.
They' (**d**) .... my friends.
He' (**e**) .... nice and she' (**f**) .... nice too.
The name of my school (**g**) .... The *Just Right* School of English. It' (**h**) .... a good school and the teachers (**i**) .... very good too. Yusef, Nadia and I (**j**) .... in the same class.

7 **Complete the sentences with subject pronouns and the correct form of the verb *be*.**

A My name (**a**) ....is.... Paul. (**b**) .... from the USA. My office (**c**) .... in this big building. (**d**) .... a computer company.

B Hi, (**e**) .... Elza. (**f**) .... pleased to meet you! (**g**) .... from Rio de Janeiro. It (**h**) .... the most beautiful city in Brazil! I (**i**) .... a student.

C What (**j**) .... your name? Where (**k**) ....you from? My name (**l**) .... Wilhelm. (**m**) .... from Austria. (**n**) .... a student.

8 **Complete the questions with *is* or *are*. Then answer the questions. Use short answers.**

a Is Paul a student? Yes, he is.

b .... his office in a big building?

....

c .... Elza and Wilhelm from Germany?

....

d .... they teachers?

....

e .... you a student?

....

UNIT 22

be: negative, interrogative

Negative	
I am not (I'm not) You are not (aren't) He/She/It is not (isn't) We are not (aren't) You are not (aren't) They are not (aren't)	Canadian.

I'm not *Canadian.*
You aren't *American.*
She isn't *British.*

Interrogative		Short answers			
		Affirmative		Negative	
Am I Are you Is he/she/it Are we Are you Are they	Mexican?	Yes,	I am. you are. he/she/it is. we are. you are they are.	No,	I'm not you aren't. he/she/it isn't. we aren't. you aren't. they aren't.

Is he British? – ***No, he isn't.***
Are they French? – ***No, they aren't.***

Do not use contractions in affirmative short answers (short answers with *yes*):
Are you Australian? – ***Yes, I am.***

1 Complete the information with words from the conversation below.

I am not = ...

are not = ...

is not = ...

MAN: Where are you from? Are you Brazilian?
WOMAN: No, I'm not. I'm Mexican.
MAN: Are Mexico and Brazil both in South America?
WOMAN: No, they aren't. Well, Brazil's in South America but Mexico isn't. It's in North America.
MAN: Oh, OK.

2 Find two questions about nationality in the conversation in Activity 1.

Question 1: ....
....
..............................?

Question 2: ....
....
..............................?

3 **Rewrite the negative forms using the contractions *I'm not*, *isn't* and *aren't*.**

a Ronaldo is not from Mexico. He's Brazilian. ....

b We are not Australian. We're South African. ....

c Are you American? – No, we are not. ....

d Are you English? – No, I am not. I am Australian. ....

e Joni and Neil are not American. They're Canadian. ....

f I am not Russian, my friend is Russian. ....

4 **Fill in the blanks.**

MAN: New neighbours?

WOMAN: Yes. Jane and Peter.

MAN: (**a**) .... are they .... ?

WOMAN: Well, she' (**b**) .... Australia, I think.

MAN: Oh, (**c**) .... he .... Australia too?

WOMAN: I don't think so.

MAN: (**d**) .... from?

WOMAN: I don't know. Let's go and say 'hello'.

5 **Complete the dialogues.**

MAN 1: Is Paris nice?

WOMAN: Sorry?

MAN 1: Paris, (**1**) .... it nice?

MAN 2: Yes, (**2**) .... is. But we (**3**) .... from Paris.

MAN 1: Oh, sorry. (**4**) .... you from then?

MAN 2: We'(**5**) .... from Chartres.

MAN 1: (**6**) .... Chartres near Paris?

WOMAN: Yes, it is.

DAVE: Hi. I (**1**) .... Dave.

GLORIA: I'm Gloria.

DAVE: Where are you from?

GLORIA: Guess!

DAVE: (**2**) .... South African?

GLORIA: No, I (**3**) ....

DAVE: Are you Canadian?

GLORIA: No, I'(**4**) .... Canadian.

DAVE: Australian?

GLORIA: That's right!

WOMAN 1: Look. This (**1**) .... my boyfriend.

WOMAN 2: (**2**) .... Canadian too?

WOMAN 1: No, he (**3**) ....

WOMAN 2: Where (**4**) .... from?

WOMAN 1: Guess!

WOMAN 2: I know! He (**5**) .... Russian, right?

WOMAN 1: Yes, he (**6**) .... ! How do you know?

WOMAN 2: It's just a guess!

6 **Look at the pictures. Correct the statements.**

Example: *Madonna's Australian.*

She isn't Australian. She's American.

you - ?

a Kimonos are Korean. ....

b Boomerangs are from South Africa. ....

c The pyramids are in Russia. ....

d The flag is French. ....

e Pizza's from France. ....

f You're British. ....

7 **Complete the conversations.**

Conversation 1

BOB: Where ...*are*... you ...*from*..., Richard?

RICHARD: I'........ Australian.

BOB: .... you .... Sydney?

RICHARD: No, I'........ . I'm .... Melbourne.

BOB: .... Melbourne near Sydney?

RICHARD: Yes, ... Well, it .... very far.

BOB: .... Sydney the capital of Australia?

RICHARD: No, it .... It'........ Canberra.

BOB: .... nice?

RICHARD: I don't know!

Conversation 2

JILL: Are Tina and Carlos in your class?

LUPE: No, ... They'........ in a different class but we'........ friends.

JILL: .... you all .... Argentina?

LUPE: No, we .... Tina and I .... from Argentina but Carlos .... He'........from Venezuela.

8 **Complete and answer the questions.**

a Who ...*are*... you?

You: I' ....

b Where .... you .... ?

You: I' ....

c What' .... your nationality?

You: I'..........

d .... colour' .... the flag of your country?

You: It'..........

e What .... the names of the countries near your country?

You: ....

f What colour .... their flags?

You: ....

g .... your favourite colour?

You: ....

h Really? That'........ my favourite colour too!

UNIT 23

there is, there are

	Singular countable noun	Uncountable noun	Plural countable noun
Affirmative	There is + a/an	There is some	There are (some)
Interrogative	Is there a/an ... ?	Is there any ... ?	Are there any ... ?
Negative	There isn't a / an	There isn't any	There aren't any

With singular countable nouns, use *there is + a/an*:
There is a computer on the table.
Is there a bathroom in the house?

With uncountable nouns, use *there is + some*:
There is some sugar on the table.

In a question about an uncountable noun, use *is there + any*:
Is there any food in the house?

With plural countable nouns, use *there are + some* and *any*:
There are (some) tomatoes in the kitchen.
There are two computers on the table.
Are there any TVs in this house?

After a question starting *is there ... ? / are there ... ?*, you can use a short answer:
Is there a lamp on the table? – Yes, there is. / No, there isn't.
Are there curtains on the windows? – Yes, there are. / No, there aren't.

1 Look at the picture and complete these sentences about what you see.

a There is a .... tomato.
b .... milk.
c .... eggs.
d .... apples.
e .... chicken.
f .... door.

2 Read the texts *a–c*. Which text matches the picture?

a There is a bed next to the door. There are no clothes on the bed and there is some milk on the desk. There are no shoes on the desk. There isn't a TV in the room.

b There is a desk next to the door. There are some clothes on the bed and there is a TV and some cheese on the desk. There aren't any shoes on the desk.

c There is a desk next to the bed. There is some bread on the bed and there are some shoes on the desk. There isn't any milk on the desk and there's no TV on the desk.

3 Complete these sentences and examples with the phrases from the boxes.

Affirmative

There is some There are some There is a

a Use .... with singular countable nouns.
.... *cat under the table.*

b Use .... with uncountable nouns.
.... *sugar on the table.*

c Use .... with plural countable nouns.
.... *eggs in the fridge.*

Negative

There isn't any There is no / There isn't a
There are no / There aren't any

d Use .... with singular countable nouns.
.... *library in the town.*

e Use .... with uncountable nouns.
.... *cheese in the fridge.*

f Use .... with plural countable nouns.
.... *shoes in the bedroom.*

4 Complete the questions with the phrases from the box.

Is there a Is there any Are there any

a .... dining room in your house?

b .... TV in your bedroom?

c .... rugs in your house?

d .... computer in your house?

e .... cheese in your fridge?

5 Answer the questions for your house. Use short answers.

Yes, there is. / No, there isn't.
Yes, there are. / No, there aren't.

a Yes, there is.

b ....

c ....

d ....

e ....

6 Complete the email with *there's* / *there are*.

To: Keith
From: Louise

Hi Keith!
I'm staying in an amazing hotel. (a) ..There are.. more than 600 rooms! (b) .... a computer in every room. And (c) .... a DVD player too, and (d) .... DVDs to borrow from a (free) library in Reception. Next to my room, (e) .... a private bathroom, and (f) .... two TVs – (g) ....one in the bedroom, of course, and (h) .... one above the bath! (i) .... big gardens all around the hotel, and (j) .... three swimming pools. (k) .... one on the rooftop! And (l) .... also a private beach just for the hotel. From my windows, (m) .... beautiful views of the beach. This is the best holiday!!

Louise

7 Find the mistakes in these sentences and correct them below.

a ~~Are~~ there a bank near here?
..Is there a bank near here?..

b There is some table in the dining room.
....

c There aren't any milk.
....

d Is there any rugs in your house?
....

e In our town there is three supermarkets.
....

f There isn't no computer in our house.
....

UNIT 24

Tense review: present simple, present continuous, past simple, future

1 **Put the time expressions in groups. Be careful! Some expressions can go in more than one group.**

Present continuous	Present simple	Past simple	*Going to* future
at the moment	at night	ago	next week

ago   at the moment   at night
at 8 o'clock   every day in 2001
last week   never   next week
now   on Sundays   soon
this week   tomorrow   usually
yesterday

2 **Complete the best man's speech with the correct form of the verbs in brackets, present continuous, present simple, past simple or *going to* future.**

Dear friends, today we **(a)** are celebrating (celebrate) Paul and Nicole's new life together. I **(b)** .... (meet) Paul on our first day at high school. We **(c)** .... (do) everything together. We **(d)** .... (study) together, we **(e)** .... (have) fun together and we **(f)** .... (not fall) in love together, but at the same time. One day he **(g)** .... (say): **(h)** '.................... (do) you .... (remember) Nicole from high school?' He **(i)** .... (not have to) say more. I **(j)** .... (know) this **(k)** .... (be) real love. So, in the future **(l)** I .... (do) everything with Paul AND Nicole! And the first thing we **(m)** .... (do) is drink to their happiness. Nicole and Paul!

She saw him at 8.00. It's now 12.00. → She saw him four hours **ago**.

Tim graduated in June. It's September now. → Tim graduated three months **ago**.

3 Study the sentences in the box. Rewrite sentences *a–d* using *ago*.

a Jan and Ben met in 1999. → They ....met a long time.... ago.

b Henry VIII died in the 16th century. → He ....

a long time ....

c Colin started his job on Monday. Today is Friday. → He

....

d Emma had breakfast at 7.00. It is now 2 o'clock. → She

....

When did you do these things? Write similar sentences about yourself.

have breakfast meet your best friend start English classes
leave home get up see a good film go on holiday

4 Fill in the blanks with the correct tense of the verbs in brackets.
Clue: look at the time expressions (underlined).

a I <u>always</u> ...get up... (get up) at 7 o'clock. (present simple)

b <u>It's 12 o'clock</u>. Why ...are... you ...getting up... (get up) so late? (present continuous)

c I ...got up... (get up) really late <u>this morning</u>. (past simple)

d <u>Tomorrow</u> ...I'm going to get up... (get up) early and go to the gym. (*going to* future)

e I .... (eat) chocolate <u>all the time</u>. It's a bad habit!

f What time .... you .... (go) to bed <u>last night</u>?

g .... you usually .... (play) football <u>on Saturdays these days</u>?

h It .... (not rain) <u>now</u>. We can go out.

i How .... you .... (get) to the party <u>tonight</u>?

j Gloria .... (move) to Australia <u>many years ago</u>.

k Sonia .... (move) to Australia <u>next year</u>.

l Thomas .... (look) for a new job <u>at the moment</u>.

5 Read the interview. Fill in the blanks with the correct form of the verbs in brackets: present simple, present continuous, past simple or *going to* future.

The interview

Emmy Hurtado, young businesswoman of the year

What does your company do?

We (**a**) buy...... (buy) beautiful objects from other countries, like rugs from Mexico and baskets from the Philippines. We (**b**) .... (sell) them in London.

What's special about your company?

We (**c**) .... (help) communities in poor countries. We (**d**) .... (pay) them a good price for their objects and we sell them at good prices here. Everybody (**e**) ....(win)!

How did your business start?

I (**f**) .... (go) to my family's village in the Philippines on holiday. I (**g**) .... (see) some beautiful baskets. I (**h**) .... (talk) to the people. They wanted to do business in other countries but they (**i**) .... (not have) enough money and they (**j**) .... (not have) any contacts. We (**k**) .... (give) them the money to start and we (**l**) .... (sell) their baskets here.

What are your plans for the future?

Next year we (**m**) .... (open) a new shop in Scotland. We (**n**) .... (look) for a place now.

6 Use these prompts to ask Emmy questions about her business. Think about the tenses you need and the question forms.

a When / you / go / to the Philippines / ?
When did you go to the Philippines ?

b you / start / your business alone / ?
.... ?

c Who / work with / you / ?
.... ?

d you / sell / things from India / ?
.... ?

e you / plan / to open more shops / ?
.... ?

f How / your business / do / at the moment / ?
.... ?

g What country / you / visit / next / ?
.... ?

h you / sell / clothes / ?
.... ?

Answer key

Unit 1

1 a once a week
b twice a month
c twice a month
d She plays tennis three times a month.
e She works out twice a week.

2 a She always reads. / She reads every day.
b They never read.
c Three times a week.
d How often does Corinne work out? / How often do Alice and Ella work out? / How often do Emma and Rich watch TV?
e How often does Corinne play football? / How often does Corinne watch TV? / How often does Charlie work out? / How often do Alice and Ella play football?
f How often does Charlie play football? / How often do Alice and Ella watch TV?
g Alice and Ella
h Emma and Rich
i Charlie
j Emma and Rich

3 a How often do you go swimming?
b How often do you read the newspaper?
c How often do you do homework?
d How often do you play tennis?
e How often do you go to the seaside?
f Do you work out every day?
g Do you always get up late at the weekend?

Unit 2

1 a 2 b 3 c 4 d 1
2 b an c – d – e an f a
3 a Ø b a, a c Ø, a, a d an e an f Ø
4 b the c a d the e the f the g the h a i the j the
5 b Ø c an d an e an f a g a h Ø i Ø j a

Unit 3

1 b Can; Yes, she can.
c Can; Yes, he can.
d Can; Yes, she can.
e can play
f can't
g can play
h can't

2 b I think Mike plays the drums, because Jay, Maggie or Helena can't play the drums.
c I think Helena plays the keyboards, because she and Mike can play the keyboards, but Mike can't read music. Helena can read music.
d I think Mike or Helena is the singer, because they can both sing.
e I think Jay or Helena writes the songs, because they can both read music.

3 b Can Ahmed's mother play the piano? No, she can't.
c Can dogs swim? Yes, they can.
d Can a cheetah run fast? Yes, it can.
e Can your parents dance the tango?
f Can you draw well?
g Can you send a text message?
h Can you speak French?
i Can you count to 100 in English?
j Can you ride a motorbike?

4 **Stevie Wonder**
can: play the keyboards (piano and synthesizer)
play the drums
play the bass guitar
play the harmonica
can't: play the trumpet
play the cello
play the violin

5 Paul McCartney is a famous musician. He can play keyboards, the drums and guitar. He cn't play the trumpet, the saxaphone or the violin.

6 b can't c can d can, can't e can, drums f can g can't, can

Unit 4

1 a 3 b 4 c 1 d 5 e 2

2 b taller than
c as thin as
d thinner than
e as modern as
f more modern than
g as interesting as / more interesting than

3 We use *-er* than when an adjective has one syllable with a short vowel sound.
We use *more … than* with adjectives which have two or more syllables.

4 b more useful than
c as useful as
d as short as
e shorter than
f bigger than
g more interesting than
h longer than
i as good as
j better than

6 b as comfortable as
c more beautiful than
d easier than
e as fast as
f more expensive than
g as expensive as
h cheaper than

7 *Sample answers:*
b The Great Pyramid is older than / not as high as the Eiffel Tower. The Eiffel Tower isn't as old as / is taller than the Great Pyramid.
c The European continent isn't as big as the American continent. The American continent is bigger than the European continent.
d Brad Pitt is as handsome / tall as George Clooney. Brad Pitt is younger than George Clooney. George Clooney isn't as young as Brad Pitt.
e Angelina Jolie is as beautiful / tall as Scarlet Johansson. Angelina Jolie is older than Scarlet Johansson. Scarlet Johansson isn't as old as Angelina Jolie.

Unit 5

1 **Countable:** sandwiches, a banana, an egg
Uncountable: bread, coffee, sugar, some meat, some chicken, cheese
2 b six
c 500g
d six
e six
f 500g
3 b How much, is there? a bowl
c How much, is there? some
d How much, is there? some
e How many, are there? about five
f How much, is there? a bottle
4 a 1 It's £4 for 1lb.
2 How much is that milk? It's 50p a litre.
3 How much are those eggs? They're £1 per dozen.
4 How much is that salad? It's £1.50 a bag.
b 1 1 lb, please.
2 How much milk do you want? A litre, please.
3 How many eggs do you want? A dozen, please.
4 How much salad do you want? A bag, please.
5 a much, much is it?
b some eggs, many do you need? much is that / are they?
6 A: some eggs, How many
B: 2
A: How much
B: 250g
A: some, How much
B: 125g
A: How much
B: 300ml
A: some, some
B: some, some
7 b much
c much
d much
e much

Unit 6

1 a these
b this
c that
d That, This
e those
f those
g These
h This
2 1 That's
2 these
3 That's
4 Those, that, this
5 those
6 those, these, those
3 1 a that b that c That's
2 d this
3 e these f This is g this h these
4 i these
5 j those k these/those
6 l these m That's
7 n this o those p that's

Unit 7

1 b F c T d T e T f F g T
2 b I'm going to be a doctor.
c I'm going to have a shower.
d They're going to crash.
3 A
b Is, going to, No, he isn't.
c Are, going to, Yes, they are.
d Is, going to, No, he isn't.
e Are, going to, No, they aren't.
f Is, going to, No, she isn't.
B
b Ben is going to book the tents.
c –
d Jamie is going to contact *Watersports Weekly*.
e Kate, Jamie and Hannah are going to write to the local newspapers.
f Hannah is going to find out about canoes at Loch Keel.

Unit 8

1 a Is she going to, is
b Is he going to, he isn't
c are you going to watch
d are we going to
2 K: Why are you going to do that?
D: I'm going to become a singer in a band.
K: How are you going to buy food?
D: I'm going to eat at my parents' house.
K: Are you going to tell them?
K: When are you going to tell them?
K: Are they going to be happy for you?
D: Yes, because I'm going to be famous!
3 b are cutting
c are building
d aren't going to have
e isn't going to have
f is going to be
g isn't going to be
h are going to have
i are going to get
4 b Is the building company going to keep the trees? No, it isn't.
c Are many people going to work in the shopping mall? No, they aren't.
d Are people in Cowden going to enjoy the shopping mall? No, they aren't.
e Are the children going to play safely? No, they aren't.
f Are the shoppers going to have a place to park their cars? Yes, they are.
5 b Is the car park going to be free?
c Is there going to be a special area for children?
d Is the shopping mall going to open on Sundays?
e Are you going to build the shopping mall this year?
6 a Cinema, Screens 1 and 2
Food Village
Concert Hall
b restaurant *Mamma Mia*
restaurant *Chinatown*
The Circle Art Gallery
7 a In the autumn.
b Who is going to play at the Concert Hall in October? *Dixiejazz*.
c When is the reggae band going to play? In September.
d What special event is there going to be at *Mamma Mia*? An ice cream week.
e How long is the special deal at *Chinatown* going to last? 8 days.
f How many new places are going to open at the Melting Pot? 3
g What month is The Circle Art Gallery going to open? In October.
h Where is the exhibition of African Art going to be? At The Circle Art Gallery.

Unit 9

1 b feed c give d drink e let f let
2 b Feed c him d Give e Let
f Don't let
3 b Don't leave
c Feed
d Give
e Don't give
f Leave
4 *Sample answers*
b Give the fish enough water.
c Change the water every week and don't forget to keep the

water clean.
d Do not put anything in the water.
e Put plants in the water to provide shelter.
f Don't put the aquarium in direct sunlight.
g Feed the fish every day, but don't give them too much food.

5 b Don't swim here.
c Turn left.
d Be careful!
e Don't play football.
f Don't wear trainers.
g Don't take drinks into the theatre.
h Wash your hands.

6 b I c O d O e I f I g O

7 b Take your dog for a walk often.
c Come!
d Give your dog food!
e Make sure you have lots of fresh water for your dog.
f Sit!
g Don't forget!

Unit 10

1 **Yes:**
stay until the bell rings
ask for permission to leave the classroom
No:
eat during class
touch other people's work
work on other subjects during art class
run in the art classroom
Not necessary:
be silent during class
stay in your seat

2 a Yes, you do.
b you have to; No, you don't.
c Do you have to; Yes, you do.
d Do you have to; Yes, you do.
e Do you have to; No, you don't.

3 b We don't HAVE to go to every class.
c They DON'T HAVE to do any homework.
d Do you HAVE TO speak French at work?
e Can you LEND me some money?
f Can I BORROW your MP3 player?

4 b doesn't have to
c must
d has to, has to
e mustn't
f must
g don't have to
h mustn't
i must
j has to

Unit 11

1 b past c past d past e present f present g past h present

2 b 'm
c 'm, 're
d was
e Were
f were, weren't
g Are
h aren't

3 a Where was Kim yesterday?
b Where were Laura and John yesterday?
c Where are Laura and John today?
d Where was Kim last week?
e Where were Laura and John last week?
f Where is Kim today?

4 b were c Was d was e was f were g is h are i isn't

5 b were c was d were e wasn't f were g were h were i was j were k weren't

6 Conversation 1 Picture B
Conversation 2 Picture A
b at the zoo
c No, he was at the zoo.
d No, they were at home.

7 a was
b Was, she was
c Were, they weren't, were having lunch
d Where was Louise at 12 o'clock?, was
e is she, is
f is she doing, 's watching TV

Unit 12

1 die died
do did
give gave
go went
have had
like liked
live lived
read read
see saw
study studied
want wanted
watch watched
work worked
write wrote
b watched, died
c lived
d worked
e read, liked
f went, saw, wrote

2 1 Lily 2 Daisy 3 Poppy
b Lily didn't sleep in her bed last night.
d Poppy felt sick all morning.
e Poppy is sick in bed.
f Lily didn't go home last night.
g Poppy didn't want to eat anything this morning.
h Daisy didn't listen to *Romance* on the radio.
i Lily can sleep all day.

4 b left
c turned
d wasn't
e continued
f found
g became
h gave
i started
j arrived
k became
l died

5 b He didn't take 200 men with him. He took 170 men.
c He didn't turn west to go round the Cape of Good Hope. He turned east.
d He didn't reach the coast north of the Cape after three years. He reached it after three months.
e The Sultan of Malindi didn't give him two Arab ships to go to India. He gave Vasco da Gama two Arab pilots.
f Vasco da Gama didn't die in Portugal. He died in India.

Unit 13

1 b Grandma's birthday
c Peter's birthday
d Pauline's music exam
e Mum's birthday
f Dad's golf tournament
g dog's vet appointment
h Daisy's drama performance
i Mum and Dad's wedding anniversary

2 b near
c in
d next to
e on
f opposite
g between

3 b Martin's shoes are
c The box
d is in the box
e between, the box

f lamp is, the desk
g is, the door
5 1 b 2 a
6 b P c Be d Be
1 c 2 b 3 d 4 a
7 b My daughter's 20.
c He's a student.
d His car's blue.
e No, he's a dentist.
f What's your brother's name? His name's Rafael.
8 b grandfather's
c Graham's
d Alice's
e Omar's
f Graham's
g Beatrice's
h Freya's

Unit 14

1 a her b their c his d his e our f our g their h your i her j my
2 2 His, c
3 My, h
4 Her, a
5 their, g
6 my, j
7 Their, b
8 our, f
9 His, d
10 Her, i
3 A
b his c He's d My e their f his
B
g your h our i you j my k Her
C
l your m They're n They o my
4 b 4 c 2 d 6 e 3 f 1
5 b Their c Our d Its e her f His g your
6 a They're
b It's, Its
c You're, Your
d He's, His
e They're, their
f He's, His
g It's, Its
h You're, your
i he's, His
j their, They're
7 b His c Its d our e their f our g her h Their

Unit 15

1 b gets up c has d doesn't have e gets up f opens g close h relax i watches j reads k don't see
2 a F b F c T d F e F f F g F
3 1 Rick
2 Paul
3 Martin and Karen
4 Clara
5 Lily
4 a sleeps
b live
c don't work
d doesn't dance, plays
e doesn't like, studies
f don't go
g doesn't see
6 b doesn't do, does
c eats, doesn't eat
d doesn't eat, hates
e loves, doesn't listen
f doesn't like, enjoys
g ski
h goes, goes
i doesn't drive, goes
j takes
k has, buys

Unit 16

1 b Do; have, eat, like, drink, eat
c Does; have watch
3 b Do, like
c Do, buy
d Does, like
e Does, drink
f Does, eat
g Do, work
h Does, have
4 b Sandy c Maiko d Sandy, Raj e Maiko f Raj g Sandy
5 b Does Sandy eat fish? No, she doesn't.
c Do Maiko and Raj eat fruit? Yes, they do.
d Does Maiko eat bread? No, she doesn't.
e Do Maiko and Raj eat a lot of rice? Yes, they do.
6 a Do people in this country eat eggs for breakfast?
b Do they like to eat a lot of meat?
c Do they drink a lot of coffee?
d Do they have a lot of fish?
e Do they like rice?
Japan
7 a Do b Do c Are d are e are f Are g Do h Do i Is j Are k Do l Are m Do n Do o Is p Does q Do r Is s Do

Unit 17

1 a 3 b 4 c 1 d 2
2 a 2
b Where does Kelly sing? 3
c Who does Kelly sing with? 1
d When does Kelly sing? 4
3 a I often go to the movies.
b Who do you go with? I usually go with my friend.
c Where does your brother go swimming? He sometimes goes to the club.
d When does he go? He always goes on Saturdays.
4 b do c does e do
5 2 a 3 d 4 c
6 b 2 c 7 d 5 e 8 f 3 g 6 h 1
7 b When do you go to the disco?
c Where do you buy your clothes?
d Why do you walk to school?
e How do you travel?
f What do you do to relax / at the weekend / in your free time?
g What time does school / work start?
h How often do you wash your hair?
8 a She works out.
b How many times a week does Patrick play soccer? Once a week.
c What do Sue and Jane do on Fridays? They go to the cinema.
d Who does Linda have lunch with on Sundays? She has lunch with her parents.
e What time does Patrick get up on a Sunday? He gets up at 9.00.
f How do Sue and Jane spend their Saturdays? They go shopping.

Unit 18

1 b Is c Are d is e are/'re f is/'s g are/'re h are/'re i am/'m j are
2 *Sample answers:*
a Molly and Marcia are eating hot dogs.
b Hank, Tyler and Mark are playing baseball.
c Hank is throwing the ball. Tyler is catching it. Mark is hitting it.
d Carlos is climbing a tree.
e Charlie and Joanna are watching the game / sitting on the bench.
f Charlie is cheering. Joanna is clapping.
3 1 A, B 2 C, D
4 b watching, 's having
c are climbing
d Are (they) watching
e 's dancing
f watching, is
g Is (Bev) climbing, isn't

h isn't going, 's going
i 're cheering
5 *Sample answers:*
b In Picture A, Jill and Andy are dancing.
In Picture B, Jill and Andy aren't dancing. Andy is driving away, and Jill is waving goodbye.
c In Picture A, Mia is walking the dog. Sam is climbing a tree, In Picture B, the dog isn't walking. It's barking at Sam in the tree.
d In Picture A, Nicky and Anna are sitting on the grass, talking and laughing.
In Picture B, Nicky and Anna aren't talking and laughing. They're playing musical instruments.
e In Picture A, Katie and Tina are playing baseball.
In Picture B, Katie and Tina aren't playing baseball. They're playing netball.
f In Picture A, Sam is climbing a tree. He is looking at the cat in the tree.
In Picture B, Sam isn't looking at the cat. He's looking at the dog barking at him.

Unit 19

1 **b** She's wearing blue trousers, a blue jacket and a white shirt.
c He's eating with Marla.
d He's wearing a grey suit and a red tie.
2 **b** What is Heather wearing?
c What is Nicole doing?
d What are Jed and Marla wearing?
3 **b** are you eating
c is she crying
d are you phoning
e are they wearing
f are you having
4 2 f 3 e 4 b 5 c 6 a
5 1
a is (he) sitting
b is (he) doing
c is having
d is (he) eating
e is (he) wearing
f is sitting
2
g are (you) doing
h 'm taking
i are (you) standing
j haven't got
6 **b** Where are you going?
I'm going to the Jazz Club.
c Who are you going with? I'm going with Lyn, Paul and Mark.
d Where are you meeting?
We're meeting at Gino's Bar.
e How are you getting there?
Pete's giving us a lift.
f What time are you coming back?
We're coming back by 1 a.m.
g Why aren't you wearing jeans?
Because we're all wearing black.

Unit 20

1 **b** PC **c** PC **d** PS **e** PS **f** PC
2 1 e PS
2 a, d PS
3 f PC
4 b, c PC
3 **b** watch
c 's making
d doesn't speak, 's taking
e don't take
f is living, lives
4 **Habits:** I never watch TV in the morning. Jack and Jenny don't take photos very often.
Facts: I usually work in an office. Sally doesn't speak French. She usually lives in Peru.
Happening at this very moment: I'm watching TV.
Happening now: I'm working at home. He's making phone calls. She's taking classes. They're using their mobile phone to take pictures. Margarita's living in Spain.
5 **b** 's living
c works
d 's working
e speaks
f doesn't speak
g 'm speaking
h 'm meeting
i 'm learning
j 'm having
6 **b** I usually live in London.
c She never has important meetings.
d Do you want to leave a message?
e It's Joe.
f Can I take a message?
7 **A** 3 **B** 2 **C** 1
8 **a** 're staying
b isn't
c 's working
d 's
e travels
f thinks
g 's shining
h 'm sitting
i wearing
j is
k 'm watching
l 're riding
m love
n 're staying
o 'm learning
p go
q 'm practising
r 'm sitting
s see
t 'm staying
u 're doing
v 'm having

Unit 21

1 **b** my name is, my name's
c he's, he is
d they are, they're
e we are, we're
f you are, you're
g it's, it is
h she's, she is
2 **A** she
B you, I, He
C We, I
D they, they, They
3 **b** is **c** are **d** are **e** am, are
5 **b** 's **c** 's **d** is **e** is **f** 're **g** 're
6 **a** m **b** is **c** is **d** re **e** s **f** s **g** is
h s **i** are **j** are
7 **A** **b** I'm **c** is **d** It's
B **e** I'm **f** I'm **g** I'm **h** 's **i** 'm
C **j** 's **k** are **l** 's **m** I'm **n** I'm
8 **b** Is; Yes, it is.
c Are; No, they aren't.
d Are; No, they aren't.
e Are; Yes, I am.

Unit 22

1 I am not = I'm not
are not = aren't
is not = isn't
2 1: Where are you from?
2 Are you Brazilian?
3 **a** Ronaldo isn't from Mexico.
b We aren't Australian.
c No, we aren't.
d No, I'm not.
e Joni and Neil aren't American.
f I'm not Russian.
4 **a** Where (are they) from?
b 's from
c is (he) from
d Where's he

5 a
1 is 2 it 3 aren't 4 Where are 5 're
6 Is
b
1 'm 2 Are you
3 'm not 4 'm not
c
1 is 2 Is he 3 isn't 4 's he 5 's 6 is

6 a Kimonos aren't Korean. They're Japanese.
b Boomerangs aren't from South Africa. They're Australian.
c The pyramids aren't in Russia. They're in Mexico.
d The flag isn't French. It's British.
e Pizza isn't from France. It's from Italy.
f I'm not British. I'm ......

7 **Conversation 1**
R: m
B: Are (you) from
R: m not, from
B: Is
R: it is, isn't
B: Is
R: isn't, s
B: Is it

Conversation 2
L: they aren't, re, re
J: Are (you all) from
L: aren't, are, isn't, s

8 b are (you) from
c s
d What, s
e are
f are
g What's
h s

Unit 23

1 b There is (some)
c There are (some)
d There aren't any
e There isn't any
f There isn't a

2 b

3 a There is a
b There is some
c There are some
d There is no / There isn't a
e There isn't any
f There are no / There aren't any

4 a Is there a
b Is there a
c Are there any
d Is there a
e Is there any

6 b There's
c There's
d there are
e There's
f there are
g there's
h there's
i There are
j there are
k There's
l there's
m there are

7 b There are some tables / There is a table in the dining room.
c There isn't any milk.
d Are there any rugs in your house?
e In our town there are three supermarkets.
f There isn't a computer / There is no computer in our house.

Unit 24

1 **Present continuous:** this week, next week, tomorrow, soon, next week, at 8 o'clock
Present simple: at 8 o'clock, never, on Sundays, usually
Past simple: yesterday, last week, at 8 o'clock, every day in 2001
***Going to* future:** tomorrow, at 8 o'clock, never, on Sundays, soon, this week

2 **b** met **c** did **d** studied **e** had
f didn't fall **g** said
h Do you remember
i didn't have to
j knew **k** was **l** 'm going to do
m 're going to do

3 b He died a long time ago.
c He started his job five days ago.
d She had breakfast seven hours ago.

4 e don't eat
f did (you) go
g Do (you usually) play
h isn't raining
i are (you) going to get / are (you) getting
j moved
k is moving / is going to move
l is looking

5 **b** sell **c** help **d** pay **e** wins
f went **g** saw **h** talked
i didn't have **j** didn't have
k gave **l** sold
m 're opening / 're going to open
n 're looking

6 b Did you start your business alone?
c Who worked with you?
d Did you sell things from India?
e Are you planning to open more shops?
f How is your business doing at the moment?
g What country are you visiting next / are you going to visit next?
h Are you going to sell clothes?

Notes